THE UNTAMED WITCH

Reclaim Your Instincts. Rewild Your Craft.
Create Your Most Powerful Magick.

LIDIA PRADAS

Author of *The Complete Grimoire*

Illustrations by Nata Vedana

FAIR WINDS

Inspiring | Educating | Creating | Entertaining

Brimming with creative inspiration, how-to projects, and useful information to enrich your everyday life, Quarto.com is a favorite destination for those pursuing their interests and passions.

27 26 25 24 23   1 2 3 4 5

ISBN: 978-0-7603-7663-8

Digital edition published in 2022
eISBN: 978-0-7603-7664-5

Library of Congress Cataloging-in-Publication Data is available.

Design: Cindy Samargia Laun
Illustration: Nata Vedana

Printed in USA
Printed in China

DISCLAIMER

*Given the limited space, I designed this book
to be as complete as possible. The information
in it derives from personal experience, folklore,
and the cited witchcraft and occultism authors.*

*Its main aim is to inform and entertain;
it does not replace professional services, in
particular those regarding safety and health
matters. Consult a professional when needed.
Check your local regulations and comply with
them, as some may interfere with some
of the information presented here.*

*The author and publisher are not responsible
for any loss or damage caused, directly or
indirectly, by the contents of this book.*

CONTENTS

CHAPTER 1

THE JOURNEY INWARD LEADS US OUTWARD

Beginning on your path as a witch can feel overwhelming. A lot of information is available, but it can be difficult to decide which sources you should trust. There are also many branches to explore, and you may have trouble differentiating between them, understanding their themes, and finding a clear way to your own path. It is not always a smooth journey.

—

Traveler, your footprints
are the only road, nothing else.
Traveler, there is no road;
you make your own path as you walk.

—ANTONIO MACHADO, *Traveler, your footprints*

—

Note: This chapter title comes from a modified sentence of the book
Rewilding: Meditations, Practices, and Skills for Awakening in Nature by Micah Mortali.

I think one of the beauties of the craft is that you are always learning and progressing. You can overcome a block by getting organized, finding a mentor, or exploring the paths until you discover what truly motivates you. But even when you are well on your way, doubts can resurface, and you may feel uncertain of your direction or find yourself on a plateau.

For me, the solution was, and is, to get confident with my reality, exploring myself first and then engaging with my surroundings to better understand how I relate with my inner and outer worlds. Knowledge of yourself and of the world around you can bring the clarity you are seeking and open new possibilities for your craft—and that is the best way to experience it.

About This Book

I conceived this book as a way for beginners to overcome their initial fears and for more advanced witches to overcome blocks. This journey will lead you to understand what the craft means for you at this moment of your life and help you to explore other aspects of your life. The book is divided into nine chapters, laid out in a progressive order that allows you to develop your craft by exploring yourself and your environment. The first chapters are shorter, and as we get deeper into the craft and how to put it into practice, they get longer.

Although I tried to write all the chapters so they are valuable to and inclusive for all types of witches, practitioners, and people curious about the craft, I think it is always

important to know an author's background because it tends to permeate their work. I was born and raised in Spain where I was fascinated by local folklore and traditions. Ever since I was a child, my mother shared her knowledge about energy work and herbalism with me. I became more interested in the occult when I grew up.

I identify as a Wiccan, and I like to define my magick as modern witchcraft, but traditional folklore and land witchcraft strongly influence my craft. I have focused on teaching Wicca and witchcraft for several years by publishing books, writing, and being active on social media. That and ecology are my passions. I focused on the latter by using my degree in environmental science and my master's in science communication.

With this project, I wanted to create a guide that allows the reader to explore what I describe in the text. My previous books, *The Complete Grimoire* and *The Path of the Witch*, explain some basic concepts more deeply, and the first book is especially helpful if you are a complete novice. However, you don't need to read them beforehand to understand and make good use of this book.

Most of the occult books that I've read are written from a personal point of view involving the writer's experiences. I have nothing against this style; in fact, some of my favorite books are written this way. But my scientific background permeates my writing style and makes me express myself in a more impersonal way. I always try to lay out information in a simple, structured way that makes it easy to comprehend, and then I add exercises that allow you to put your new knowledge into practice.

My style doesn't make this book less intimate. Here you will find the flesh and bones of my craft, what nurtures my beliefs. My witchcraft path and my spiritual beliefs are deeply intertwined, and I present them in that way. This being said, I want this to be a book that works for witches of all backgrounds, so I make sure to establish the origins of beliefs, so you can decide if a path resonates with you or do more research if necessary.

I aimed this book especially at the solitary practitioner who seeks a personal connection with the craft. I do mention some practices that can or should be carried out in group rituals. In these instances, the focus is on joining forces for an objective. The main premise stays the same: access your power without intermediaries.

I'm a firm believer that practice makes perfect. For me, it would make no sense to simply share information without a way for you to try to use it or corroborate it. So, you will find exercises that allow you to internalize the knowledge in this book and put the information into practice as you work through each chapter.

Finally, this is not a book of spells; rather, it is designed to help you create the pillars that will sustain your craft. Keep in mind that the basics are not something that only beginners do; they are the foundations of magick, and they are the fundamentals of the practices for both beginner witches and those who are more advanced.

Witchcraft and Magick

Witches are practitioners of magick. The occultist Aleister Crowley coined the spelling of *magick* with a *k* to differentiate the art of illusion from the craft, a practice of interacting with magick and entities to create change.[1]

There more than one definition that fits the word *witchcraft*. I like to define it as the ability to modify the energetic threads that connect everything to create a desired change. Through time, people have developed many ways to approach witchcraft. For some, it is intertwined with spirituality; others see it as an art, something completely secular.

One of the best depictions of magick comes from the author Ann-Marie Gallagher. She describes reality as a web of multidimensional threads that connect everything (see page 14). The threads are physical, but the connections they establish are not. We can use our physical and energetic actions to modify the threads and thus change the relationships.

Approaches to Witchcraft
There are many techniques for practicing magick and changing fate, and how the concept of "magick" is understood depends on cultural background, traditions, and folklore. It is also tied to the type of energy that you use to create change (e.g., spirits, the elements, or planets). Two of the most common divisions are high or low magick and left-hand or right-hand paths.

The Journey Inward Leads Us Outward

High magick is also known as ceremonial magick, and it involves complex and detailed rituals. Before they can participate, practitioners are often expected to make extensive preparation, including reaching certain levels of knowledge, attaining mastery of techniques, and being part of a coven for several years. Low magick, often considered witchcraft, features a simpler approach, using what you have available for the craft and relying on more commonly accessible folk knowledge.

Occultists are still debating the difference between left-hand and right-hand paths. Some practitioners associate the left-hand path with baneful techniques and the right-hand path with benevolent methods.

For others, the left-hand path simply implies accepting both darkness and light, separating it from morals and ethics.

There isn't one "right" way to do magick. In my experience, the best approach is to get to know many branches of magick and try the ones that fit your vision of the world and your lifestyle. This will give you a more comprehensive view of how energy interacts and creates change. Low magick has always worked better for me, but I have included a couple of high-magick techniques in my craft. Duality has a strong role in my magick, but my methods often stick to the right-hand path. This is what I have found works for me; when you explore, you will find your own way.

Witchcraft is not the right path for people who come looking for a "quick fix" or "ancient secrets." Witchcraft is art, practice, discipline, knowledge, and passion. Only by working on yourself and exploring the world around you will you discover your own path, the truth that lies in you.

One of the most common concerns about witchcraft is its cost. In my experience, the truth is that it does come with one. When you ask something of magick, it's not simply a matter of making a request; you need to put effort and energy into mastering the craft. It's an exchange. Not all rituals will work for you, and some rituals that do won't always work in a way that satisfies you. You will need to decide what fits your craft and what is worth it for you.

There is another cost of witchcraft, and that is that it sticks with you. Your experience of the world changes you, and you cannot return to the way you saw it before. That knowledge—and your new understandings of the world and yourself—become part of who you are.

Energy Surrounds Us

Energy has a central role in witchcraft. Many cultures have studied the energy that welds reality. As it is intangible, we can only access it via experimentation and observing its effects on the tangible world. Most knowledge about spiritual energy comes from unverified personal gnosis (or UPG).

Some people have an easier time perceiving energy than others do; they are often called psychics, empaths, highly sensitive people, or other similar classifications. However, you don't need to have a gift to sense and use magick in your craft. It is a skill that can be learned and developed with time and practice.

Taoism identifies qi as the energy of life, present in everything. It divides it into the duality of yin and yang, which permeates all aspects of life.

ENERGETIC DUALITY CORRESPONDENCES

Yin	Yang
Receptive	Projective/active
Negative	Positive
Darkness	Light
Earth	Heaven
Cold	Heat
Wetness	Dryness
Flexible	Solid

The division of dualities creates a human reality composed of three energies: telluric energy (yin), celestial energy (yang), and energy that flows through our body, which I call "inner energy."[2] You can also interact with the qi of the elements that surround you to receive information and align it to match your desires.

The Journey Inward Leads Us Outward

CONNECTING WITH YOUR INNER ENERGY

In the Taoist interpretation, life force is stored in a point called *dantian*. The dantian is divided into the lower dantian, middle dantian, and upper dantian, which draws a parallel with the trifold of the soul (see page 25).

The lower dantian is located at the belly, two finger widths below the navel. Energy stored in the lower dantian is called *jing*, the rawest energy of the body. Jing travels to the middle dantian, in the middle of the chest, and gets transformed into qi, the energy that fuels our body. When qi is refined, it becomes *shen*, which travels to the center of the head, the upper dantian, and promotes thinking, manifestation, memory, and the like.[2]

A healthy flow and replenishment of the energy in the dantian is vital to using your inner energy. One of the most common ways to accomplish this is with controlled breathing.[2, 4] Breathing moves the energy inside our bodies by following what's called the *microcosmic orbit*, a circuit that goes from the belly to the top of the head and then back to the belly.

Control Your Breathing

Go to a place where you won't be interrupted, preferably a place where you can stand barefoot. Having your feet in the soil and your head toward the sky will create a connection with telluric and celestial energies.

Adopt a straight posture with a neutral spine that allows you to align the three points.

Focus on your breathing, using your diaphragm and belly to move the lower dantian. Place your hands over your belly and feel the energy inside it moving and replenishing. Repeat this step for five to ten minutes.

Move your hands to the middle dantian. Breathe with your chest, mobilizing the energy's transformation into qi. Keep doing this for five to ten minutes.

When you feel ready, move to the upper dantian. Start doing complete breaths, filling both your belly and your chest, with one hand placed over each point. Feel how the energy is pushed up and replenishes your entire body.

RECEIVING AND PROJECTING ENERGY

Our bodies can receive and project energy. Receiving is also often called channeling. Channeling exterior energy creates an energetic bond with the external source that feeds you that force. Projecting energy consists of freeing that energy or your energy toward a goal.

Hands are one of the most common ways to direct energy. At the center of the palm, under the middle finger, we find the *laogong*, or palace of labor, point. This acupuncture/acupressure point, sometimes considered a minor chakra, is a main energy door and an easy place to detect energy.[2]

Direct the Energy Within You

Begin by holding two palm-sized rocks, one in each hand. Take your time and become familiar with their energy, shape, weight, and other characteristics. Allow yourself to enter a calm state of mind.

Now, visualize an energy flow from one stone to your hand, through your body, to your other hand, and finally to the other stone. Synchronize that flow with your breathing: take energy when you breathe in and project it when you breathe out.

Keep practicing until this flow becomes smooth. If you aren't exhausted, try inverting the energy flow to further strengthen your ability to direct your energy.

IDENTIFY YOUR PROJECTIVE AND RECEPTIVE HANDS

We each tend to have a hand that is more suitable for projecting and a hand that is more for channeling, although both can be trained. To identify your receiving and projecting hands, clasp your hands together. The thumb that naturally lands on top is the projecting hand.

Telluric energy is the energy generated by the earth, including what we experience with our senses (e.g., soil, life, and elements) and what we don't (e.g., magnetic fields, atmospheric reactions, and gravity). Some places on our planet have stronger telluric energy than others; these are called hot spots (see page 134).

Cosmic energy reaches the earth from the stars and other celestial bodies in the universe. It might seem as if cosmic energy is more potent than telluric energy because its source is bigger. However, they are equally important; consider the proximity of the earth, directly affecting us, as well as its being the source of our life.

Finally, your inner energy is the energy that belongs to your body. According to Taoism, your qi comes from two sources: your progenitors, who gave you the first sparkle of qi, and your surroundings. Your body processes your qi and the energy from your environment and creates the inner energy that flows through your body.

Energy work is a big part of witchcraft, and it is essential to identify the energies that surround us and how they affect us. Still, it is most important to understand how our energy behaves and how to control it. When we classify energy, we often use adjectives that relate to other senses, such as cold, warm, wet, or dense.[3] This approach makes it easier to identify specific types of energy, as we don't have words in our vocabulary for the exact intangible feelings they produce in our bodies.

The Web of Fate

The web of fate is a metaphor used to illustrate the concept of the energetic links that connect everything. Magick work is based on modifying these invisible links to change our reality and adapting it to a more desirable outcome.[5] This concept implies that fate can be changed. It is not written in stone; it is not unavoidable and inevitable, something that has to be accepted and can't be changed. Instead, this comes closer to a Nordic philosophy, in which people can affect their fate to some extent with their decisions.[6] We are given a particular set of conditions at the beginning of our life, but we can still act over them.

When you are studying the web of fate, it is crucial to understand that changing the web will always have an effect. Keep in mind that the result may be the one that you desired, or it may not, and this effect, in turn, has consequences, both good and bad.

There is some debate about this and the fairness of your actions. For example, casting a spell to get a job may mean a more qualified person won't get it. However, being more fun than that person can also lead to you getting the job instead of them. Witchcraft is like other abilities that can give you an advantage; how you use your advantage will depend on your moral compass. For me, the vital point is taking responsibility: Your magickal actions are your actions and are tied to you (see page 172).

The Journey Inward Leads Us Outward

CHAPTER 2

REWILDING

The term rewilding was born in the green radical movements of the late twentieth century.[7] Rewilding's primary purpose is to allow nature to return to its predomesticated state by recreating an area's conditions before human intervention and letting it regain its natural balance. This method focuses on studying ecosystems to determine which main elements are missing from their chains and reintroducing those elements in controlled environments. As the bigger problems are solved, the changes this creates will also ease the smaller problems, and equilibrium will be reestablished.[8]

—

Rewild / ri: 'waild/

Verb

To make wild again.
To restore to a natural state by enabling
natural processes to repair damages.

—

When we apply the concept of rewilding to the craft, we get a spirituality that aims to return to our roots—revisiting the basics of the mind–body–soul–environment relationship to rebuild the craft. Following a parallel with environmental movements, it is focused on understanding key elements of the craft and then allowing them to run their course.

In a world dominated by technology and external stimuli, this type of witchcraft focuses on understanding the slow pace of the universe and discovering your truth. It is a path that you can walk only through observation, experimentation, and awareness. Trusting your intuition can seem like a leap of faith, but it is based on complex research and practice. It's a long-term journey of self-understanding and learning about the world.

Nature, Humans, and Witchcraft

As civilization progresses, we tend to spend more time indoors. As a result, many people experience a disconnection from Nature, community, and even themselves.[9] We have generated the illusion that there is a separation between Nature and humans, as if we are not a part of a whole.

Many witchcraft and pagan traditions have a strong link with Nature. They don't all necessarily worship it, but they all have a deep connection to the natural world. Many of their philosophies and beliefs agree that we are Nature and Nature is us. Understanding this means feeling connected with Nature and creating a bond with it. The advance of technology

has deepened the significance of this issue because it is easier to feel disconnected from natural cycles when you live in a bubble of cement in a city.[10] Some neo-pagan traditions have experienced a rebound because of people's attempts to fight the disconnection; this can result in overmystifying some practices and places. The truth is that all Nature is sacred.

Creating a relationship with Nature takes time and effort. Nature is out there for us; we need to take the initiative. There are many ways to do this, from understanding its cycles and relationships to interacting directly with it by walking barefoot on the grass, bathing in a stream, or enjoying sunbeams (see page 99). I firmly believe that if you want to create a bond, you must be proactive in protecting Nature in the ways that are possible within your means. We can't summon Nature's power while causing it harm.

Environmental impacts have always taken their toll on humanity, sometimes in a more noticeable way than others. Climate change has evidenced with overwhelming examples that our actions have consequences. However, in some circles, the notion that humans and Nature are the same still seems radical. And, although it is true that all living beings alter their environment—rabbits dig holes, elephants take down trees, plants break stones with their roots—the current changes caused by humans that we are witnessing are too fast and severe. Humanity's changes have been far more severe during the last century than they have before, and environmental dynamics cannot assimilate them.[11]

BAREFOOT GROUNDING

Grounding is an exercise that allows us to stay more fully present in our lives. It strengthens our link to the current moment we are experiencing. There are different ways to practice grounding (see page 176), but direct connection with the Earth is one of the strongest ones.

There is an entrance for telluric energy on the soles of our feet called *yongquan*, or gushing spring.[2] Absorbing the stabilizing energy of the Earth helps us get grounded. Plus, walking barefoot has many other benefits, such as improving the balance of our body, strengthening muscles, and maintaining a good range of motion.

Grounding Yourself

To practice grounding, find a quiet place without any sharp or slippery objects—a beach is usually one favorite for beginners. Remove your shoes and start walking. Focus on all the movements that your feet are making, including how they bend and recover. Focus on how the parts of your foot that were a prisoner of the shoe are activated. Feel the texture of the ground on your skin.

The movement becomes more natural as you walk, but don't stop thinking about it. Focus a bit more and feel how the energy enters through your soles and is transported into your body's circuit. Feel how the movement of your body pushes energy and puts it into circulation.

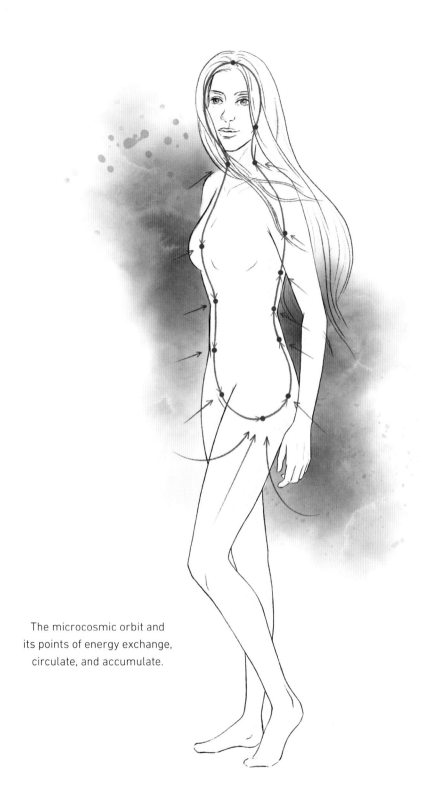

The microcosmic orbit and
its points of energy exchange,
circulate, and accumulate.

Connecting with Nature in the City

I have discussed the importance of identifying and working on the connection between humans and Nature and how an urban way of life can work against us. However, many witches live in cities, either out of necessity or because they like it. That doesn't mean they can't restore their bond with Nature; there are several ways to connect with Mother Earth.

Get rid of the idea that cities are barren lands away from Nature. The truth is Nature is always present in every place on the Earth. You are Nature. Learning how to find these connections inside the city will help you immensely:

- Identify your local flora and fauna. In a city, you can find many species of trees and grasses and different types of birds, insects, and small animals. Local parks often offer free courses or guided tours to teach you how to identify them.

- Surround yourself with plants. Grow herbs or vegetables in pots, or decorate your home with indoor plants. Participate in a community garden if your city allows it.

- Pay attention to the weather. Learn about the changes related to each season and feel how the energy changes with the weather (see page 166).

- Get in touch with celestial energy and cycles. The energy of the sun, the moon, and other celestial bodies can be felt everywhere.

- Join a group of people with the same interests as you. There are many group activities that you can join to feel more connected with Nature, from eco-activism to outdoor sport or bird watching.

- Incorporate eco-friendly changes into your life. Many people feel more in tune with Nature if they feel they are actively working to protect it.

Mind, Body, Soul

The number three appears repeatedly in many sacred texts across different cultures. It is fairly common to find sacred trinities that explain our reality (past, present, and future), human nature (mind, body, and soul), or the divine (triple deities such as Hecate, the fates, or the Holy Trinity).

The division between mind/soul and body finds its roots in ancient Greek philosophy, with Aristotle's and Plato's works as key representatives. It was later developed by other philosophers such as Saint Thomas Aquinas and René Descartes. Later came the Christian trialism doctrine, dividing the idea of mind/soul into two separate concepts with the mind being our thoughts and the soul being the divine in us.

The alchemist Paracelsus developed the idea of three primes, or *tria prima*, that merge to create everything. The three aspects were sulfur or combustible, mercury or volatile, and salt or noncombustible, nonvolatile matter. When applied to humans and our reality, this is the result:

THE THREE PRIMES AND THEIR CORRESPONDENCES

	Sulfur	Mercury	Salt
Principle	Combustibility	Volatility	Solid
Human Aspect	Soul	Mind/Spirit	Body
Element	Fire	Air	Earth/Water

The philosopher John Cottingham introduced the idea of mind–body–sensation, substituting the soul for the emotions that we experience. However, modern witchcraft conserves soul and includes emotions in the aspects of mind and soul. The witchcraft author Aidan Wachter defines the trinity of the body, mind, and soul as a vehicle with two riders; mind and soul intertwine and affect how our body experiences the world, but they are not the same.

It is important to recognize the effects that magick has on the practitioner. Mind, body, and soul aren't isolated elements. The connection between them and their relationships interact with each other. Some studies are starting to highlight that the physical state can affect the mental state and vice versa.[12]

Once you start working with energies of a certain level, they will affect the unbalanced regions of your body, mind, and soul. The type of impact is usually related to the kind of energy that you were invoking. However, the change is not always predictable.[13] Once you learn to identify the signs that the energy creates in you and the imbalances that you need to address, you will be able to start aligning your power.

An imbalance cannot be ignored; it is already creating change. Going against it will make it harmful. Instead, you need to redirect it toward the desired outcome.

Body

Some types of spirituality present the Divine as a separate concept from the mundane. For example, according to Christian beliefs, our bodies are mere vessels that hold our souls during our limited time on Earth until we reach eternal life.

Paganism embraces Nature and the physical world as intrinsically spiritual. In the trinity of our existence, the body is the only physical part. It was created in this realm and will stay here after death. Our body is our connection with the land, and because of it, it is inherently sacred.[14]

We experience our surroundings through our bodies. They are our gateway to the marvels of the universe, but they also set our limitations. Movement and actions are often key parts of rituals. Many psychic experiences come to us through our physical senses; we experience energy through our bodies and create change.

Our body has ways to communicate with our mind, and it often acts as a bridge between our soul and our mind. Learning to understand its signals, such as the gut feeling, is a powerful tool for the craft and ultimately for knowing yourself. Accepting our strengths and weaknesses are vital to moving forward in our path. I usually include mental health as a part of body health, not mind health. Our brains are an organ as any other, so they can be sick and malfunction, requiring medication or rehabilitation (therapy). It's also important to remember that health is not our primary goal for our bodies; it is the maintenance we need to perform to enjoy their full potential.

Understanding that our body is sacred means learning to take good care of it, but it also means being gentle with it. It means abandoning harmful habits and pursuing health in an enjoyable way. Not everybody has the same tools or opportunities to take care of their bodies. It is unfair, but they should not feel ashamed about it. Sometimes we can only do so much to tend our health.

Mind

The mind is often seen as our consciousness. It is our personality, how we present ourselves to others, how we act when we are alone, our thoughts, our memories, and our imaginations. Part of our mind and personality is innate, but many other parts result from our education and past experiences. It is not unusual for our minds to change and adapt over time. As we advance through our life, our mind is able to shift its perspective and adjust to new circumstances and information.

Some people oppose this change and think "I am who I am" or "old people are set on their ways" or similar limiting beliefs. However, I think that the adaptability of the mind is one of our best gifts. It is like a muscle; the more you broaden your horizons, the more you will want to explore.

Another advantage that the mind gives us is rationalizing things and creating plans. Critical thinking is a must in the craft; check the sources of the information you are given, question the reasons behind your behavior, and analyze the science and history behind the practices.

Keep in mind that it is not good to rationalize everything; sometimes you just need to feel. Emotions are also part of who we are, and they give us relevant information about why things affect us the way they do.

In the book *Weaving Fate*, Aidan Wachter insists on the importance of putting effort into clarifying what our real actual state is and what is influenced by what our mind wants to believe based on ideals, expectations, and past experiences.[15] This takes a lot of introspection and personal work. Our mind is programmed to make connections.[16, 17] In the wild, mammals survive by linking a sound or a smell to the presence of a threat. Our brain still does the same; it looks for recognizable patterns that have been useful in the past and applies them to the current situation. Sometimes we need to take a step back and think about whether we are making decisions based on extrapolations of our mind and if they are plausible or correct.

Soul

The presence of a soul is the mark of living beings, and a soul does not disappear after death but migrates. In ancient Greece, Homeric poems describe the nature of the soul as something a person "loses" in death as it departs to the Underworld. The word used for *soul* is also translated as "being alive," so the interpretation could be either "when someone dies, they lose their soul" or "when someone dies, they stop being alive."[18]

As the theory of the soul developed, the soul acquired more attributes. In *De Anima*, Aristotle describes it as the abilities that perform all living beings' living functions, substantiating the theory that the soul is incorporeal. On the other hand, Plato describes the soul as an immortal trinity: reason, spirit, and appetite.

Aristotle and Plato developed theories about the multiplicity of the soul in a hierarchical order. The first soul makes the being grow, and plants, animals, and people all have it. The second soul, shared by animals and people, allows them to perceive pain, pleasure, and desire. Lastly, the third soul represents reasoning, and only people have it.

This triple division of the soul repeatedly appears throughout history and in different cultures, although the names and attributes change slightly. Within pagan communities, they are often referred to as "the three cauldrons" in reference to the cauldrons mentioned in "The Cauldron of Poesy," an Irish poem from the seventh century CE.

It divides the soul into the cauldron of warming, the cauldron of motion, and the cauldron of wisdom.

Laura Tempest Zakroff, in her book *The Witch's Cauldron*, describes the symbolism of these items in the craft.[19] Cauldrons were common tools at home, near the hearth, for feeding and warming the household. They represent how the magick in the mundane is seen in witchcraft. The cauldron of warming is situated in the lower abdomen/pelvic region, in an upright position, containing the basic instincts and abilities we need to live. The cauldron of motion is found in the chest, tipped or in its side, containing our passions and hopes. The cauldron of wisdom, found in the head in an upside-down position, contains our spirituality.

In this representation, each soul is believed to exist in a different realm, acting as "samples" of these realms in our physical existence.[3] The cauldron of warming is ruled by the Underworld, the cauldron of motion is ruled by the Midworld, and the cauldron of wisdom is ruled by the Upperworld. (For more information about the realms, see page 77).

Other traditions also explore this trinity of the self. In modern witchcraft, the concept of high, middle, and lower selves has grown in popularity. Although there are parallelisms between these terms, they are not the same, as the selves relate to the person as a whole and not just the soul (see page 37).

MIND-BODY-SOUL-ENVIRONMENT ALIGNMENT

Modified from "El libro de las pequeñas revoluciones" by Elsa Punset.[20]

Balancing the different parts that form you will allow you to develop them equally, giving you a more comprehensive vision of yourself and your surroundings. These aspects need to be in balance before you can align them. From there, you can focus them on a goal or intention. This exercise helps you understand your balance in a graphic way and then apply the appropriate practices you can use to reach alignment.

Understanding Your Balance

Begin by taking time to reflect on each of the following four elements:

Body: Have you stopped to think about how your body is? Are there any parts that require special care? Are there parts that make you proud? When was the last time that you scanned it and focused on the sensations and information that it gives you?

Mind: Focus on your train of thought. How are your thoughts? Are they fast? Slow? Positive? Negative?

Soul: What ignites your soul? What inspires you? What makes you want to act, to improve? What freezes your soul and brings you doubts? When was the last time you did something that fueled your spirit?

Environment: What's your relationship with your surroundings and with nature? Are you a tidy person? Do you enjoy being outdoors? Do you notice the seasonal changes? Do you always follow the same route when going somewhere?

Now draw a circle and divide it into four equal parts, one for each element. Draw a point for each field—the closer to the center, the more important that area has in your life. Join the points to create a wheel. Will it roll?

It's likely that your wheel is unbalanced. Remember, your balance is key here, and it is a necessary first step. You cannot align the four aspects toward a common goal if one of them is underdeveloped. Deep meditation and other practices can help, but alignment will never happen without balance.

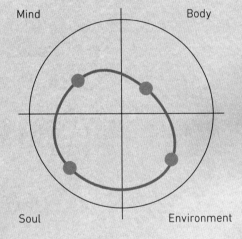

WAYS TO ALIGN YOURSELF

Field	Aligning Practices
Body	Exercise, body scan, auto-massage, taking care of ailments, flexibility training
Mind	Journaling, listening to your emotions, reading, mind exercises, practicing assertiveness, setting healthy boundaries
Soul	Finding inspiration, discovering hobbies you are passionate about, learning about philosophy, learning about spirituality
Environment	Decluttering, exploring your city/town, spending time outdoors, learning about nature and your surroundings

Skills in the Wilderness

The craft is called "the craft" because it is something you create. I believe that getting in touch with the origin of the materials you use is a powerful way to increase your connection with your magick.

The tools that you use in your craft are the physical elements you use to modify the threads of fate. Knowing their origins is a key skill if you want to increase your connection with them and improve the productivity of your craft. Much in the same way that food that you grow yourself tastes better, the materials that you know from the very beginning will better match your craft. I don't want to dismiss the power of tools, materials, and ingredients bought and not grown, gathered, or made. However, it is essential to get them from a reliable seller. Don't be afraid to ask about their origins and the process that brought them to you.

By working on your self-reliance, you strengthen your mind–body–soul connection. Your mind plans and learns the process, your body carries it out, and part of your soul and your energy gets imbued in the final result. This process can seem intimidating at first, but the truth is that it can consist of small actions, some of which you may even be doing already! Also, there is no need to master all of them or do it all simultaneously. Enjoy the process.

Grow or Forage Your Herbs

By growing your herbs, you not only know their source, but you can also grow them with a particular intention in mind. Plus, knowing the products that have been used in growing them is always important. Cultivating plants may seem complicated, but many of them are beginner friendly. For example, you will find kits for culinary herbs.

Some plants are not usually grown at home or found in shops. For those, foraging is a good option if you have enough botanical knowledge. Check your local laws before foraging plants, and observe the rules that ensure a better environment for everybody (see page 105).

Find Your Crystals

This one can be more difficult. Some minerals can only be found in particular parts of the globe, so there isn't much we can do to find them where we are located. However, some are relatively easy to find. Quartz, for example, is abundant in many places and can be found if you have some training and know what to look for. Plus, quartz is one of the most versatile crystals.

Apart from crystals, keep in mind that you can also use stones. They may be less "fancy" or "trendy," but they are equally powerful and have been used in witchcraft rites for centuries. In folklore, stones have particular uses depending on their shape and color; for example, hag stones (which see the Otherworld through their holes) and stones with a line that wraps around them grant wishes.

Create Clothing with Knot and Symbol Magick

Knot magick consists of securing your intention with every knot you make. It is usually done with string, but the same idea can be applied to other material. Because of this, knitting, sewing, embroidery, and crocheting are great candidates for this type of magick. "Love in every stitch" takes on a new meaning in the craft. The thing you imbue with knot magick needs not be exclusively dedicated to the craft. This technique is appreciated by those who prefer to live their craft discreetly.

Make Your Own Tools

Although some witches prefer to work without tools, they are essential to many practices. Tools allow us to control energy with more precision or modify and boost it to match our needs. They are also highly symbolic, which aids in elevating the meaning of the ritual. Because of this, they are consecrated and treated as sacred objects.

Tools are also helpful in the mundane part of magickal workings. The knife used to cut herbs, the knitting needles used for knot magick, and the chalice used to drink during a ritual have physical uses, but their meanings are still magickal (see page 140).

Cook

Kitchen magick is often conceived of as a type of witchcraft in itself. This branch mixes the art of cooking with witchcraft by incorporating symbolism and correspondences into food and recipes. The ingredients and methods are chosen according to their flavors and also their magickal correspondences, allowing you to adapt each recipe to a particular situation or intention. I go deeper into kitchen witchcraft in *The Path of the Witch*.[21]

Cooking is also a great way to nurture your body. Healthy eating habits ensure that your body has the nutrients it needs to function well. It is not unusual to encounter practitioners who benefit from the healing properties of food to add herbalism to their dishes.

Witchcraft and Rules

The topic of the rules of witchcraft has been widely discussed in the occult community. Some practitioners defend the existence of universal laws that affect all actions that tap into magick. By contrast, for other practitioners, the rules that apply to you highly depend on the type of magick or spirituality you work with. The following are some of the most popular rules in modern witchcraft. It doesn't mean that you need to apply them all to your craft. Your craft should match your ethics and morals (see page 172).

The Wiccan Rede and the Three-Fold Law
Two of the rules that most Wiccan branches share are the Wiccan Rede and the Three-Fold Law. Both emanate from the concept of not using witchcraft to hurt others, leaving some practices such as cursing or hexing outside the Wiccan craft.

Other traditions that do not follow these rules have explored such practices and do not see them as against their guidelines.

The Wiccan Rede is often cited as "An ye harm none, do what ye will," although this is only a part of the complete poem. The authorship date of the poem is not clear; it is believed to be written between 1960 and 1970. The Rede refers to pursuing your desires if it doesn't damage others. However, some Wiccans interpret this with a less passive point of view: as an encouragement to do good, as inaction can also cause pain.

The Rule of Three or Three-Fold Law states that everything you do will come back to you multiplied by three. Some variations disregard the three-aspect, saying that the energy you put into the world comes back to you as it is, good or bad.

These rules are seen as the Wiccan version of the Golden Rule, an axiom found in many religions around the globe that refers to treating others how you want to be treated. Some practices fall in a gray area when talking about these rules. The discussion is often focused on free will. All our actions affect others, some of them more than others. Practices such as binding a person to prevent them from doing something are often debated, as they can be used to protect yourself or to harm another person.

—

**Your craft should match
your ethics and morals.**

—

The Powers of the Sphinx

The powers of the sphinx, sometimes presented as the witches' pyramid, are a set of rules in ceremonial magick initially laid out by Éliphas Lévi and then expanded by Aleister Crowley. Although they have been primarily studied in Thelemic contexts, they have also been adopted by other traditions such as some branches of Wicca.

This philosophy is visually represented as a squared-based pyramid with a total of five points and five rules: The bottom four points are to know, to dare, to will, and to keep silent, and the top point is to go. These rules have their own correspondences, but they can slightly change depending on the source.

To know means that the process of learning is never-ending because there is always new knowledge that you can incorporate into your practice. To know doesn't stop there; it also means knowing yourself, understanding your limitations, being honest with yourself, and finding your true intention.

To dare is interpreted as stepping out of our comfort zone and trying new things, exploring and practicing what we have learned. To learn new skills, you need to put them into practice and overcome the fear of failing.

To will refers to persevering. It means having the willpower necessary to keep going when the initial motivation wears out. To overcome obstacles, you need to be consistent and persevere through your journey; it is the only way to create change.

To keep silent reminds us that some things should be kept only between us and the powers we work with. It also refers not to outing pagans without their consent, as, sadly, it can put them in danger. I think it's important to distinguish between keeping your practice private, teaching, and fighting to remove the stigma from pagan practices. All of these activities can be compatible.

To go is added after the first four are already established in the transformation—the point at which we have accomplished all the previous steps and we start the learning cycle again. It is seen as a connection with the divine, with the quintessence. These rules are often presented as a series of steps that allows us to move forward in balance. The only way to achieve the fifth step is to conquer the first four: "In order to DARE we must KNOW; in order to WILL, we must DARE; we must WILL to possess empire, and to reign, we must BE SILENT."[22]

The Blacktree system, a tradition of sabbatic witchcraft, added a sixth element, to grow, creating the witch's hexagram.[23] This axiom represents the step after you put your new knowledge into practice: adapting, making the information yours, and developing your own ways. As a step, to grow would be placed between to dare and to keep silent. Three lines of equal length represent the witch's hexagram crossed at the center. This symbol is also used as a way to map our reality (see page 86).

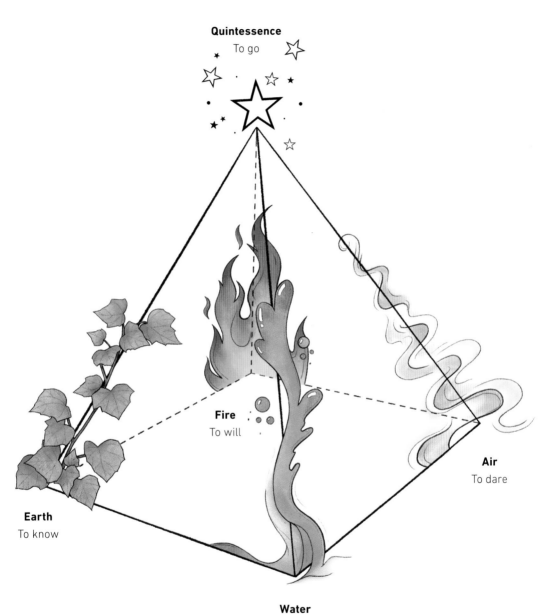

Quintessence
To go

Fire
To will

Air
To dare

Earth
To know

Water
To keep silent

CHAPTER 3

SWITCHING CONSCIOUSNESS

W ho we are and how we relate to others and to our surroundings depends on our personality and experiences. To explore ourselves and our connections with this and the Otherworld, we often use the system of the three selves. The lower, middle, and higher selves represent how we interiorize events and connect with the outside world.

—

The ship wherein Theseus and the youth of Athens returned from Crete had thirty oars, and was preserved by the Athenians down even to the time of Demetrius Phalereus, for they took away the old planks as they decayed, putting in new and stronger timber in their places, in so much that this ship became a standing example among the philosophers, for the logical question of things that grow; one side holding that the ship remained the same, and the other contending that it was not the same.

—PLUTARCH, *Theseus*

—

We are not fully aware of what the three selves see. That's why we need to dig and find it out through exercises and activities. Although not everything processed by the three selves goes through our conscious mind, consciousness is how we interact with our surroundings. Understanding the ways that the three selves filter our experiences will help us understand how our consciousness reacts. This will also help us focus our magickal workings on the most appropriate level of consciousness for what we want to do.

The Lower Self, Middle Self, and Higher Self

The three selves, or the three minds, is a classification system that divides our human experience into three differentiated parts: the lower self, the middle self, and the higher self. This division is often related to the three realities of the soul (see page 22). This system is influenced by the archetypes described in Jungian psychology (see page 38), religions such as Christianity or Hinduism, and even New Age movements.

The middle self is what we call "ourselves," our conscious mind that perceives the world, plans, and reacts. It is how we present ourselves to the world. It is viewed as rational and analytical, but that doesn't mean it doesn't experience feelings. However, emotions don't present themselves raw as they would in the lower self; they are filtered.

The lower self is considered our primal, animal self. It is not bound to our perception, representing our subconscious and unconscious. It can be regarded as the doorway to our psychic development, where intuition resides.[24] It can process information that you aren't aware of.

The higher self connects us with divinity. It is often called a super consciousness or a personal divine.[24] It is not bound to linear time, as it is eternal and sees past, present, and future. Some traditions believe this is the only part of our soul that survives death and travels to the other world or reincarnates. The lower, middle, and higher selves create parallelism with the three realms: the Underworld, the Midworld, and the Upperworld. In the same way the *axis mundi* connects the realms, the selves are aligned and connected (see page 78). There are similarities with the triplicity of the soul as well (see page 25). Each balances the others and perceives different parts of the same reality; all of them are necessary for our existence.

The perception of each self is distinct, and in turn our approach and work for each should also be different. That said, as we perceive our higher self and our lower self through our middle self, it is important to recognize we decode these messages through the lenses of our cultural background and previous experiences.

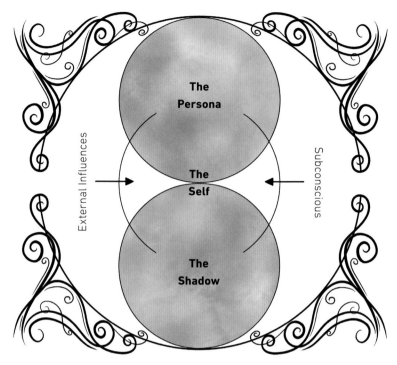

The Persona

External Influences

The Self

Subconscious

The Shadow

Adapted from the Jungian model of the psyche

Shadow Work

The concept of the shadow self comes from the work of the psychiatrist Carl Jung, who focused on this concept and how it is reflected in our life. Jung considered the "light" our conscious or how we present ourselves, while the "shadow" is what is occult, our subconscious.

Jung's model of the mind is a self-regulating system that seeks balance between its main components. The Ego would be considered our conscious mind, while the subconscious would be made of different archetypes:

The Persona: The persona is our "mask." It is how we present ourselves to the outer world. This is the image of ourselves that we show.

The Shadow: The shadow is all the aspects we prefer to hide, ignore, or suppress from ourselves.

The Anima/Animus: This archetype stems from the male/female dichotomy, coming from your personal experience of gender, expectations, and experiences with other genders.

The Self: This part is the complete experience that unifies all archetypes present in a mind.

Note that the shadow is not simply or exclusively made of negative traits (as Freud suggested). It is what we reject and suppress. A person might see their own kindness as weakness and hide it, for example. The problem is that, even when suppressed, the shadow still affects who we are and how we relate to our surroundings. Ignoring it has a negative impact, as we cannot eliminate it, and our subconscious will find an alternate way to make it reach the surface.

Some common signs that something in your subconscious needs to be addressed are triggers and projection. Triggers are topics that prompt disproportionate negative responses, and projection means spotting in others, truly or in our mind construction, a behavior that we don't like in ourselves. Both create a distorted version of reality.

Shadow work is the conscious action of exploring our shadow self to understand it and assimilate it as a part of our consciousness. It has many benefits, as reincorporating the shadow self will create a stronger conscious that allows us to have better relationships, perception, emotional maturity, and enhanced energy.

Shadow work can be a challenging experience, as you can stumble upon painful events such as suppressed memories or trauma. If done incorrectly, it can be harmful and deepen that trauma. Because of that, if you suspect these things might arise, it is better to do it under the supervision of a mental health professional.

Incorporating the shadow helps solidify our beliefs and improve how we make judgments. It can also strengthen your craft and help you to understand whether something in your unconscious mind is blocking your energy and preventing you from working with it as you desire. It's also important to keep in mind that assimilating the shadow is a continuous journey without a defined end. Some parts, such as evil, can be more complicated than others, but they will manifest in more destructive ways if they are ignored. The difficult aspects need to be acknowledged so you can deal with them.

Extrasensory Perception and Psychic Development

There is a voice, a feeling present in everybody, that tells us when something is wrong, right, or simply off without tangible information about why we are reaching that conclusion. That is our intuition. It is deeply connected with our higher self, allowing us to interpret signals that our middle self doesn't detect.

Intuition should be differentiated from instinct. Instincts are fixed patterns of behavior that come from our lower selves. They are part of our animal nature, and they are often related to our survival; for example, dodging a hit is an instinct. Intuition includes processing information through our middle self and interpreting extrasensorial stimuli with a more rational mind.[25]

Intuition is often the gateway to psychic development, although some occultists recognize them as different disciplines. Psychic abilities arise from intuition to a certain point, but they are separate fields, in the same way as calligraphy and illustration share artistry in their origins.

Our body communicates with our mind through physical sensations, including the information obtained from extrasensory perception. It is vital to learn to interpret those signals to improve your psychic development. Ivo Dominguez Jr. describes this mind–body–perception relationship in his book *Keys to Perception*: "Inner senses are decoded and interpreted through your physical senses, efforts to focus more of your mental processes on sharpening the physical senses also refine the inner senses. Perception occurs in the mind, and by clearing and brightening the mind, we open more fully to our inner senses."[26]

Many methods can help clear the mind (see page 47), but it may take some exploration to find a technique that works well for you. Each brain, body, and mind is different, so it can take time to discover what slows down your thoughts. Be patient with it and enjoy the process.

In the same way that people are born with particular talents, it is common for witches to prefer a particular channel of mind–body communication. This doesn't mean they cannot develop and improve other psychic senses, but it will take time and practice, as does any other discipline. It is also important to observe psychic development and other practices of the craft with an open but critical mind. It is the only way to advance in the practice without being deceived. A study published in *Psychological Reports* showed that psychic practitioners have the same rational thinking as nonbelievers and have a higher internal locus of control than nonbelievers do. At the same time, the believers who weren't involved in the practice were more prone to intuitive thinking.[27]

Ivo Dominguez Jr. also created a division for psychic senses between clairs and noirs, from the French words for "clear" and "black."[26] Clairs are the psychic senses experienced through consciousness. They are powerful and complex, but they are also somewhat more accessible because they allow you to analyze the information with your conscious mind while you are experiencing it. Noirs are experienced through the unconsciousness and often are more suitable for advanced practitioners, as your subconscious or even entities are channeling directly through you to present the information. As the name noir suggests, you don't understand the information until it is in front of you. For example, with automatic writing, you don't know what you are writing until you finish the session and analyze it.

Humans rely heavily on their sight and hearing, and the clear senses related to these senses are the most common ones. Clair senses may tie in with recurring experiences: For example, an entity might always announce its presence with the same scent as a way to make them easier to recognize.

Other abilities are often included in this group because they are experienced through consciousness despite not being perceived through the physical senses (e.g., hearing, touch, taste):

- Claircognizance: Clear knowing. This skill allows people to "receive" true information—information there was no way they could have accessed—without a source. It doesn't mean strongly suspecting something; it is recognizing a piece of truthful information, but without knowing why you know it.

- Clairsentience: Clear feeling. When a person experiences this sense, they suddenly feel an emotion without an external reason. The information they receive is processed viscerally.

- Clairempathy: Clair emotion. Also called empaths, people with clairempathy can sense or mirror emotions from other people and feel them as their own.

CLAIR SENSES
The clair senses are experienced through the physical senses. They are:

- Clairvoyance: Clear seeing. This is the ability to see with your mind's eye. It could be in the form of mental images and symbols or as a "top layer" over what you actually see, such as auras.

- Clairaudience: Clear hearing. This skill ranges from hearing soft noises to hearing words without a clear source. It can also be experienced inside your mind, in a similar way to your internal dialogue.

- Clairtangency: Clear touching. Information can present in two ways: receiving it when you touch an object or a person or feeling a touch/pressure, such as fabric on your skin and even pain or pleasure without an explanation.

- Clairalience: Clear smelling. Having this skill means being able to smell things that others can't and even without using your nose. It is strongly related to clairgustance, and it is not unusual for them to act in synergy.

- Clairgustance: Clear tasting. This is defined as suddenly tasting something without an apparent reason. The taste can trigger memories or give you information about your current situation, depending on whether it is good or bad.

Note: Be careful when exploring the clair senses, as sudden changes in your senses can be a sign of illnesses. For example, people with parosmia might perceive everyday things as foul scents.

Sometimes clairempathy is confused with clairsentience or highly sensitive people (HSP), but clairsentients receive all types of information, not only human states, emotionally. HSP receive information from their environment faster than other people, which helps them figure out things, such as emotions, quickly also, but they don't feel them as theirs.

It is not unusual for clair and noir senses to communicate so it is easier for you, or the person the message is meant for, to interpret a message. For example, if the ghost of a person you remember as always smoking wants to contact you, it is probable that you will smell cigarettes.

GET USED TO YOUR SENSES
Getting in touch with the mundane reactions of your senses to stimuli is one of the best ways to train your clair senses. Focus all your attention on one of your senses for a few minutes and register the stimuli you detect. Reflect on their intensity and the effect they have on you.

Consciousness States

Knowing and understanding your three selves allow you to connect with your inner senses and psychic perception. All three selves are of equal importance, as they address different areas. Aligning and working with them is the gateway to progress along your path.

Humans perceive the energy that surrounds us in different ways. Some rely on interpreting the information they receive through their five physical senses, while others focus on deeper senses such as intuition or the mind's eye. Many of these states of consciousness depend on or are related to brain wave frequencies, which can also be applied to psychic senses.[28, 3, 24] Neurons' electrical pulses create brain waves to communicate between them. They are divided into bandwidths measured in hertz; the higher the brain activity, the higher the hertz.

Brain waves are often studied individually, but in reality, they are better described as a continuous spectrum. Different brain waves can be observed simultaneously in different parts of the brain, and their locations might also have different implications. Six types of brain waves have been identified, although only the first five are related to mental states.[28]

HUMAN BRAIN WAVES

Name	Hertz	Definition
Gamma	38 to 42 Hz	Gamma waves were considered brain noise at first, but they serve to pass information quickly. They are also perceived when observing acts of love or accessing transcendental enlightenment. The mind needs to be quiet to access these waves.
Beta	12 to 38 Hz	Beta waves usually dominate our brain waves. They are present during activities that require being alert, solving problems, engaging with others, or making decisions. They can be further split into high-beta, beta, and low-beta.
Alpha	8 to 12 Hz	Alpha waves occur during relaxed states, daydreaming, and flowing thoughts. They are experienced during mindfulness, grounding, and other mind–body exercises. They are the calm state of the brain.
Theta	3 to 8 Hz	Theta waves are the intuition waves. We experience them before and after falling asleep. They minimize external stimuli and focus on insight. They are experienced during deep meditation, light sleep, dreaming, and deep visualization. They help consolidate knowledge and connect you with your intuition.
Delta	0.5 to 3 Hz	Delta waves are detected during dreamless sleep and deep meditation. They suspend external awareness and promote the healing of the body.
Infra-low	< 0.5 Hz	Infra-low waves are not well known as they are difficult to measure. They are thought to control timing and neural network function.

The optimal mental state for magickal work varies depending on the work you want to conduct. Learning techniques to affect your brain waves and swift consciousness is a practice found in many spiritual practices worldwide. Most require knowledge and training. When in doubt, contact a person specializing in the particular practice that interests you.

Switching Consciousness

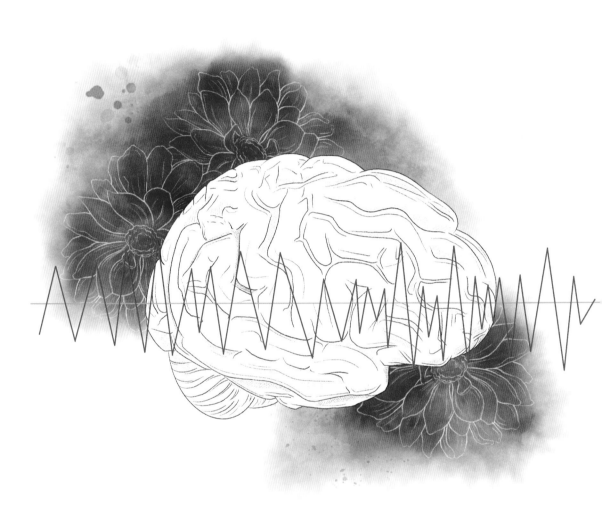

BREATHING LIGHT

Modified from "El libro de las pequeñas revoluciones" by Elsa Punset.[20]

There isn't an exact way to measure brain waves without the use of specialized equipment. However, we can train our bodies to identify the signals. When doing an exercise related to a brain wave, always begin by stopping for a moment and doing a couple of full breaths, engaging the belly, diaphragm, and chest. This will help clear your mind and relax your body so you can more easily notice the signals and identify them.

Visualizing the Airflow

First, focus on the airflow that comes into and out of your body as you breathe. Think about it as a flow of light. What color is it? Colors have different wavelengths, just as brain waves do. Our minds will use them to classify and identify other mental states.

Try this with different wavelength states, different activities of the same wavelength, and so on, and keep a record to see the relationship between those colors and your mental state. Once you have associated a color with a particular mental state, your subconscious will make you visualize it every time you are experiencing that wavelength, even if you are not consciously sure of which state your mind is in. This exercise is beneficial to use to check if you are in the right state before a ritual.

The Eightfold Path

The Eightfold Path, or Ways to the Centre, are eight methods for performing magick described by Gerald Gardner in *The Gardnerian Book of Shadows*.[29] It consists of eight techniques used to modify the state of consciousness to facilitate working with energy and magick. Christopher Penczak introduced an alternative version of this list that included the division between inhibitory and exhibitory practices, meaning slowing down the body and mind to swift consciousness or raising energy and the body's awareness through stimulation to swift consciousness, respectively.

Although Gardner numbered them, he did not specify if the eight followed an order of importance—except for the first one, Intent, which he considered essential in every operation. I have focused on the original list and included the inhibitory/exhibitory classification, as I find it extremely helpful.

1. Meditation or Concentration, Also Called Intent
INHIBITORY

Gardner describes this point with a focus on visualization: "forming a mental image of what is desired, and forcing yourself to see that it is fulfilled, with the fierce belief and knowledge that it can and will be fulfilled, and that you will go on willing till you force it to be fulfilled."[29]

This has evolved to include two different techniques: consolidating your intent and meditative states. Consolidating your intent means sorting out your real goal, the real motivation behind it, and the consequences it will bring. Sometimes this can take a lot of self-reflection, or it may be easy to establish. You need to be able to visualize it, work for it in the magickal and mundane spheres, and trust your work and the universe.

Meditative states refer to relaxed states that allow you to clear your mind of clutter, remove distractions, and be present. Different techniques enable this state, including visualization, repetitive chants, grounding, and mindfulness, among others. Although meditations are mainly inhibitory, in rare cases they can be exhibitory.

2. Trance and Projection of the Astral
INHIBITORY

Trance is a semiconscious state characterized by lack of self-awareness and absence or partial response to external stimuli. It is often conceived as a deep meditative state, almost between awake and asleep. Theta brain waves can be appreciated during trance.

There are different ways induce this state. Some are natural, such as lucid dreaming, while others are intentional, such as rhythmic repetition, hypnosis, strobing lights, yoga, surfing, and sensory deprivation. Isolation and fasting are sometimes included in this list as inhibitory practices to promote contemplation and reflection. For others, they are just ways to achieve trance.

3. Rites, Chants, Spells, Runes, Charms
DEPENDS ON THE RITE

This point refers to what is considered "witchcraft" in the eyes of the general public. All options use a language of symbols to communicate with the subconscious and the universe, thus allowing you to manifest your intent.[30]

Chants and other types of music can alter the state of consciousness depending on their beat and tone. Words can also be used as a symbolic system, representing ideas. They are a powerful tool, as they can simultaneously be symbols and create rhythm.

4. Substances That Release the Spirit
DEPENDS ON THE SUBSTANCE

Many cultures have practices that induce altered states of consciousness through the use of substances, ranging from scents and incense to alcohol, hallucinogens, and other toxins. This point can be controversial as their components or the states they produce can be highly addictive and harmful for our wellbeing.

Taking care of physical vessels is vital, and because of this I don't incorporate substances that I know will adversely affect my health into my craft. However, the truth is that this technique exists and is widespread in some circles, and some practitioners find it helpful. I think it needs to be addressed from an informed viewpoint and not ignored or avoided. These substances need to be used in a safe environment, used with caution, and never abused.

5. The Dance and Kindred Practices
EXHIBITORY

Different types of dance have been incorporated in many rituals throughout history and with different intentions, but always focused on connecting with the Divine. Dancing has also become a social activity that tightens bonds and can help raise energy as a group. This doesn't mean that it is not appropriate for solitary practitioners—dancing by yourself has the same applications.

Other types of movement and workouts are also included in this technique. Some disciplines, such as yoga, qi gong, and some martial arts, have developed exercises that focus on energy detection and control, and they improve the mind–body connection.

6. Blood Control (the Cords), Breath Control, and Kindred Practices
USUALLY INHIBITORY

Blood and breath have been present in many occult practices for centuries, as they were considered some of the mysteries that keep us alive. Breathing techniques are an effective way to change your mental state. Calm breathing relaxes the mind, while agitated breathing promotes anxious states. Because of this, breathing is key in practices such as meditation, trance, and movement.

7. The Scourge
EXHIBITORY

This point includes all types of pain-related practices, from scourge to piercings and tattoos. The scourge is a whip made of many cords used in some traditions to represent the will to learn, the pain in life, and determination in the face of adversity. A kiss often accompanies it. This practice is not intended to break the skin but rather to draw blood to the surface and promote trance.[24] This point should never be viewed as a way of punishment, only as a tool for altering consciousness. Whatever is used to release the Spirit can be a source of danger if used incorrectly; it should always be done safely.

8. The Great Rite

EXHIBITORY

In Gardnerian Wicca, the great rite describes sex between a consenting couple after they summon the gods into their bodies. Channeling the god into your body is called drawing down the sun, and channeling the goddess is called drawing down the moon. The channeling of the gods can be done independent of gender and sexuality, and it can also be done for masturbation rituals.

The great rite is more than just a sexual act; it is the communion of universal energies. There are many ways to explore it. Information and consent are vital in all practices, particularly in this one. It should always be done willingly and without coercion. Also, observe the recommendations for safe sex.

According to Gardner, you may combine many of the points into the one experiment, "the more, the better."[29] However, he also recognizes that some techniques are incompatible, and they cannot all be combined in one rite. As you have probably realized, some of these practices also entail risks. Use them with caution and guidance and always consent to them freely, without external pressure or coercion. If done incorrectly, they can be very harmful.

Gardner's description of the eightfold path has influenced modern eastern occult practices; however, many of these techniques are present in other belief systems and were perfected by different cultures. If you are interested in reading more about these techniques and their origins, I recommend *The Witch's Eight Paths of Power* by Lady Sable Aradia.[30]

Visualization

The first point of the eightfold path highlights the importance of visualization in the use of magick. It is the process of tuning a specific idea into a clear mental image.[31] To create a change, we need to be able to experience it clearly in our mind. The choice of the word experience is not accidental here. Visualization is more than just "seeing" the object in your mind. It means re-creating every aspect of it inside your thoughts, from its shape to its scent, texture, and energy. Visualization is the most precise description of your intention that you can create.

It should be noted that is not the visualization that creates the change. The visualization is what sends the message to our subconscious, or the forces that we are working with, to create the exact change that we have set with our intention. Do your visualizations. Without them, magick can find other (undesired) paths for achieving your goal.

VISUALIZATION

To train your visualization abilities holistically, choose an object that can be experienced though the five senses. In this exercise, we will use calendula, an orange edible flower, popular in the craft for its healing properties and links with solar energy.

Experience the Flower

Pick up the flower and hold it gently between your hands. Look at it closely.

Is the flower soft? Is it sticky? Does it have a certain scent? How would you describe its color? How many petals does it have? How do the petals taste? Spicy? Sweet?

Try rotating it and moving it around in the space of your mind. You should be able to appreciate the flower from different points of view. Bring it closer to you and farther away. Appreciate the details that make it unique.

Once you have mastered the visualization of simple items, move on to more complex ones, or even try visualizing energy and situations.

MIND SCREENS

Note: Have you stopped to think where you create these images? They often appear in the same spatial region of the mind. It is often located slightly in front and on top of our heads. Mat Auryn calls it "the screen of your mind."[3] Locating it will help you improve your visualization.

Exploring the Liminal

The word liminal refers to the transitional or initial stages of something. Witches are often described as explorers of the liminal, meaning they walk the space between the conscious and the subconscious minds, between worlds, and between being awake and being asleep. Liminality is used to access things out of our reach in our mundane activities. Not all realms are accessible, and not all realms are simple to enter. Some will be easier to work with than others.

There are different ways to get in touch with the liminal, but they often fall into one of these categories:

- **Rituals and techniques:** Rituals and techniques are a way to alter your state of consciousness, thus unblocking the access to parts such as the subconscious. They can also grant the ability to travel to other realms through trance, lucid dreaming, and meditation.

- **Places:** Some places, such as thresholds, crossroads, doorways, shores, beaches, and caves, are more likely than others to have this liminal energy and ease our connection with it.

- **Times:** Particular dates or moments of the day increase the connection between realms; for example, Beltane, Samhain, dawn, and dusk.

Exploring the liminal can be an intense experience. Some precautions, such as cleaning and protecting yourself beforehand to avoid vulnerabilities or always approaching them in a focused and calm state, can make your travel easier.[32] Precautions will prevent entities in the Otherworld from getting attached to you, draining your energy, or exploiting your vulnerable points. They will also ensure that you have a smooth travel back to the mundane world, and that unwanted presences don't cross with you.

CHAPTER 4

THE CYCLE OF LIFE

W hen we pay attention to our surroundings, we see patterns and cycles. Our mind is designed for this, as being able to identify patterns means being able to predict their outcomes and make the safest choice.[16, 17] Most ancient religions and beliefs focused on Mother Earth and the cyclical changes she experienced, as their survival depended on this series of events.

—

There are two sisters: One gives birth to the other and she, in turn, gives birth to the first. Who are they?

Answer: Day and Night

—SECOND RIDDLE OF
THE SPHINX OF OEDIPUS MYTH

—

Many processes in our human experience and in the universe are cyclical. Moon phases, biorhythms, water, nutrient cycles . . . they all have periodical phases that set the pace of our world. This repetition of events affects life and makes life possible. Earth cycles were the measure of time before the existence of calendars and clocks: Things were done when they were meant to be done, not on a particular date. Reclaiming this more flexible way of approaching things can boost the power of your rituals by improving their timing.

Life, Death, and Rebirth

Death is still seen as a taboo topic in many cultures. We think about the end of our life when we have a brush with death, such as the death of a close person, an accident, or an illness; most other times it often goes unnoticed, or better said, ignored.

Death is scary because it is unknown, and what we don't understand frightens us. Dying means ceasing to exist in the only world that our consciousness has ever known. Even for people who don't believe it is the end of the journey, the reality of what happens after is a mystery. You can't go to the other side just to experiment with it and then come back to life. Nevertheless, death is an undeniable truth of our experience in the mundane world. Living beings are born, live, and die, only for the cycle to repeat.

Many cultures have theorized about what happens after our time in the mundane realm runs out. The concept of soul—an ethereal part of life that only seems linked

to the Midworld by the physical body— raises the question of what happens when the physical part disappears. Does the soul dissipate the same way the body decomposes? Does it go somewhere else when it is no longer tied to a physical frame?

Following his triple division of the soul (see page 22), Aristotle stated that the first two souls disappear with the body, as they are linked to its physical presence. However, the rational soul wasn't attached to the body and survived it, migrating to a new one.

In his book *Psychic Witch*, Mat Auryn describes a division of the soul based on the three selves.[3] Upon death, the lower self comes back to the Underworld to merge with the all of the ancestors, the collective consciousness, and serve as guidance for future generations. If the collective rejects it, it becomes a "poltergeist" that resides in the Midworld, draining energy from living beings.

The middle self returns to the land of the Midworld, and its energy dissolves into the earth to protect it. If the land rejects it, it can become a ghost linked to a particular physical place.

The upper self is the only part of the soul that remains and reincarnates. Its connection with the divine collective allows it to keep the information learned in that life and share it with the rest of upper selves. The reincarnation cycle ends when the lower, middle, and upper selves find a perfect alignment in life, creating a bond between the three of them.

ACCEPTING THE IDEA OF DEATH

Grief and death are painful concepts. Western society often treats them as taboo topics in an attempt to avoid one-time suffering. This usually has the contrary effect, deepening and lengthening suffering. Getting comfortable with the idea of death is an inevitable step toward accepting our life in all its aspects. This meditation seeks to find guidance in our ancestors to come to terms with it.

For this meditation we use water, one of the most common metaphors for life. The river flow is unstoppable, just as time is; it is constantly being born at a spring and dying at sea. The same water that creates the ocean becomes the rain in the mountains. Some of these aspects make the element water the door to the Underworld (see page 80).

You Will Need
- A quiet place with a stream or a river
- An item that belonged to a loved one who has passed away (optional)

How to Do It

Look for a place with a stream or a river. Once you arrive at the desired place, walk around it to get familiar with it. Find a pleasant spot to sit where you can hear the water even feel the light humidity in the air.

Sit down and focus on your breathing and being conscious of your body and the sensations around you.

If you've brought an item with you, take it between your hands and call for an ancestor to comfort you during this meditation. If you don't have one in mind, call the collective consciousness.

Think about death without judgment or sadness. Focus on it as an inevitable event, but neither good nor bad. Acknowledge the pain that grief brings as the materialization of our love for other people.

Now focus on your body and how it keeps us alive. With happiness, accept the changes that age brings, allowing you to experience the world for one more day.

When you are ready, thank and dismiss your ancestor. Thank the stream, open your eyes, and walk away.

Rites of Passage

To celebrate the cycle of life, many cultures have developed celebrations around especially important moments in a human life. Some of the most popular are birth, entering into adulthood, marriage, childbirth, and death. Some religions incorporate their own rites for both life achievements and spiritual achievements. They are a way to reinforce the connection between beliefs and human nature. The way these events are celebrated depends a lot on the culture; I always like to underscore the idea that they need to be voluntary and safe.

Seasonal Cycles

When we think about nature's cycles, some of the first things that come to our mind are the seasons. I find it extremely beautiful how the sunlight's angle of incidence determines the flow of life over a rocky planet almost 150 million kilometers away.

Many cultures worshipped the sun as the source of life on Earth, and it represented the death and rebirth cycle. But our star was, and is, more than that. It became our way to measure time, via day and night, and the seasons; and it is our way to define directions, establishing the four cardinal points.

The season has a big impact on human life, and over the years, people have linked seasons to different correspondences to harmonize their activities with the energy of nature. The season is often seen as a metaphor of duality, a tug-of-war between light and darkness that is in complete balance and never reaches a resolution.

Four pivotal points mark these changes in places that experience the four seasons: the solstices and the equinoxes. Due to the inclination of the Earth's axis, the northern hemisphere and the southern hemisphere experience the opposite seasons. As the astronomical time and our calendar don't match perfectly, their exact dates change slightly.

The solstices are the moments when the Earth's axis is tilted most closely toward the sun. The hemisphere closer to the sun will experience the summer solstice, while the other hemisphere will observe the winter solstice. The solstices are the time of the year with the most significant difference between day hours and night hours.

During the equinoxes, the sun is exactly above the equator, and daytime and nighttime last the same amount of time. There are two equinoxes in a year, the spring or vernal equinox and the autumn equinox.

Astrologically speaking, the equinoxes and the solstices are days of high energy. They are particularly relevant in workings related to balance, light, and darkness. As they were celebrated by some ancient cultures, some practitioners also see them as a way to connect with their ancestors and their roots.

These dates do not always match the flow of nature. For example, although winter starts in late December and ends in late March, the winter months are often considered December, January, and February. Don't let yourself be constrained by the established dates; follow the rhythm that best corresponds to your surroundings.

SOLSTICE AND EQUINOX DATES	Northern Hemisphere	Southern Hemisphere
Spring equinox	March 21	September 21
Summer solstice	June 21	December 21
Autumn equinox	September 21	March 21
Winter solstice	December 21	June 21

Four Seasons, Four Energies

Each season has its correspondences based on traditional agricultural activities, our circadian rhythms, natural changes, and the energy differences experienced between them. Arin Murphy-Hiscock classifies the seasons into different tides that draw a parallelism with the phases that we experience in our life in the process of learning and growing:

- Spring: the growing tide
- Summer: the reaping tide
- Autumn: the resting tide
- Winter: the cleansing tide[33]

Spring brings new and rejuvenated energy. Nature is awakening from her winter sleep, and the light wins its battle against darkness. It invites us to start new projects, be carefree, and dream about the future. It is the moment to go back outside, rekindle friendships, and celebrate life.

Summer arrives with overwhelming energy. It is a moment of expansion when we can put into motion what we have been working on during spring. It is related to a powerful, vital, and playful energy, but also to hard work. It pushes us to keep moving forward to grow and ripen our projects, inviting us to let ourselves follow its energy.

The Cycle of Life

Autumn soothes the effervescence of summer in a way. It is the moment to harvest the fruits of our work and weigh our actions. As darkness reclaims its place, we remember those that are no longer with us. It is a time to celebrate what we have accomplished and remember the good times. As nature prepares to rest for winter, we also need to rest.

Winter is often linked to the end of cycles. Nature goes to her apparent death only to be rebirthed in spring. It is the season of resting and reflecting on our actions during the year. Winter makes us appreciate what really matters. It is the time to cleanse and let go of what no longer serves us so we can begin the year with restored energies and lessons learned.

The Wheel of the Year

The Wheel of the Year is a relatively new system used to celebrate the seasons based on reconstructions of ancient rituals, folk traditions, and new interpretations of the seasons and the solstices. The origins of the modern Wheel of the Year can be found in the 1950s in the writings of Wiccan and neodruidic authors. Nowadays, it is observed by many neo-pagans.

The Wheel observes eight festivities, or sabbats, divided into greater sabbats and lesser sabbats. This classification doesn't refer to the importance of the sabbats but more to their origins.

The greater sabbats are those inspired by the Celtic fire festivals: Imbolc, Beltane, Lughnasadh, and Samhain. They were the first additions to the Wheel by Gerald Gardner in his book *Witchcraft Today*. The greater sabbats are also called the cross-quarter days because if we picture the year as a wheel, they fall on the four cardinal points. Cross-quarter days also refers to their falling in the middle of a season, although the current dates are slightly off for this.

The lesser sabbats—Yule, Ostara, Litha, and Mabon—celebrate the solstices and equinoxes. After the greater sabbats were introduced, some covens started celebrating the equinoxes and solstices too. Their names and celebrations were officially established between 1960 and 1970.

As the main objective of the Wheel of the Year is to follow the changes in nature, the sabbats have opposite dates in the northern and southern hemispheres. The festivals of the Wheel are not exclusive to Wicca, but Wiccan dates are the most popularized ones. Many witches who don't follow Wiccan traditions have adopted this system of festivities. Some practitioners also modify it to include local festivals or to make it fit their climate.

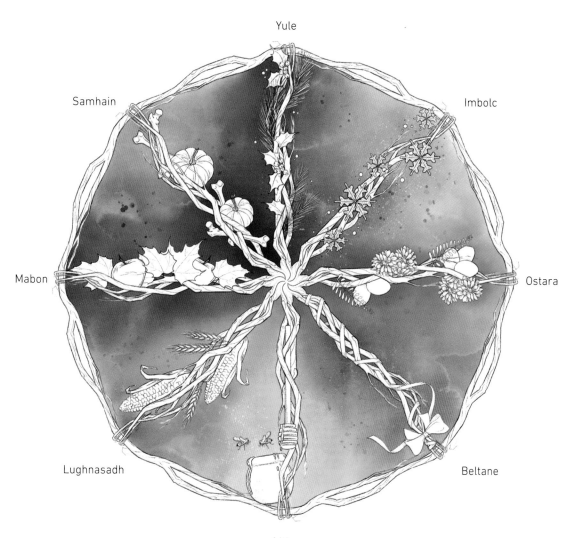

Yule

Samhain

Imbolc

Mabon

Ostara

Lughnasadh

Beltane

Litha

WHEEL OF THE YEAR FESTIVALS

Sabbat	Type	Event	Northern Hemisphere	Southern Hemisphere
Yule	Lesser sabbat	Winter solstice	December 20–23	June 20–30
Imbolc	Greater sabbat	Midwinter	February 1	August 1
Ostara	Lesser sabbat	Spring equinox	March 20–23	September 20–23
Beltane	Greater sabbat	Mid-spring	May 1	October 31
Litha	Lesser sabbat	Summer solstice	June 20–30	December 20–23
Lughnasadh	Greater sabbat	Midsummer	August 1	February 1
Mabon	Lesser sabbat	Autumn equinox	September 20–23	March 20–23
Samhain	Greater sabbat	Mid-autumn	October 31	May 1

Yule

The winter solstice celebrates the shortest day of the year, but also the return of the light. Starting from this day, daytime will be longer, but there are many cold days ahead because winter is just starting. It celebrates that nature is only asleep, not dead, and that the spring will wake her up. It is a festival related to enjoying the company of your loved ones, resting, and reflecting on your past decisions.

Yule is often seen as the sun's rebirth, and it is observed with joy. Activities include lighting candles, setting up a Yule tree, making wreaths with evergreens, or decorating a Yule log. Many traditional celebrations are similar to Christmas, as the Church adopted many celebrations from pagans.

Imbolc

Midwinter marks the coolest days of the year, but we can start to appreciate that daylight is getting longer. Snow covers everything like a white blanket, and the stored food for the winter might run low. However, sheep and goats give birth to their offspring and lactate. Because of this, milk is particularly relevant during Imbolc. The goddess Brigid is a popular deity during this time of the year.

Imbolc is considered auspicious for divination. Winter brings silence and reflection, preparing the atmosphere to connect with our psychic senses. It is also the celebration chosen by many pagans as a time to clean and tidy their homes in preparation for spring.

Ostara

The spring equinox is consecrated to and named after the goddess Eostre.[34] This period focuses on the awakening of Mother Earth and the beginning of the spring. The sun makes its presence noticeable, and the last snow begins to melt to reveal the young sprouts.

As an equinox, it focuses on the balance between light and darkness and how to reflect it in our lives. Symbols representing renewal, rebirth, and fertility, such as eggs and hares or rabbits, can be found in many celebrations.

Beltane

The fertility theme foregrounded during Ostara will fully materialize at mid-spring. Now new leaves are growing, the first fruits are ripening, and animals are having babies. It also marks the beginning of the light half of the year, the period when the light is considered to rule over darkness.

Beltane, also known as May Day, is often seen as a celebration of love, sexuality, beauty, and fertility. It is a date that many pagans choose for handfasting or weddings. It is also considered auspicious for working with entities of the Otherworld, particularly faeries and nature spirits. Flowers and bows are two of the strongest symbols of this sabbat, and they are part of many rituals and decorations.

Litha

The summer solstice marks the longest day of the year. It is the triumph of light. Litha falls between seeding and harvesting; daytime is long, and night is warm. It is the perfect time to celebrate life before going back to work. Starting from this day, the darkness will begin to reclaim its throne, but there is still a long time before the dark half of the year is upon us.

Litha focuses on celebrating life and enjoying the small things. It is common to gather around bonfires to illuminate the shortest night of the year. Many herbs with magickal properties are harvested during Litha to unlock all their powers.

Lughnasadh

Also known as Lammas, Lughnasadh marks the beginning of the harvest, particularly the cereal harvest. Around this date, wheat, barley, and corn start to turn golden under the summer sun. Many pagans use this sabbat to dry fruits under its light. In Anglo-Saxon countries, the festival also matches the time for fairs.

Lughnasadh is consecrated to the Irish sun god Lugh, but other solar deities are revered too. It is often seen as a death and rebirth period; grain dies so we can eat, but it will be planted and sprout again in spring. As grains are a big part of these celebrations, bread is a focal point during Lughnasadh.

Mabon

The autumn equinox was named after the Mabon ap Modron from an old Welsh story.[34] Mabon is also called the second harvest, as many fruits and vegetables are ripening and ready to be stored for the winter. Because of this, the cornucopia, a symbol of abundance, is a common representation for this sabbat.

As with Litha, the equinox is a time for balance. Night and day last the same amount of time, and we start approaching the dark half of the year. This swift change is bittersweet: We celebrate abundance, but it will come to an end. It is a celebration of the hard work that receives its recompense.

Samhain

The last harvest of the year is considered the end and the beginning of the year. It marks the beginning of the dark half of the year as the Wheel turns once again. It is a celebration of the cycle of life. The harvest is ending, but there are still many things to

The Cycle of Life

gather, such as squashes, berries, and fruits. Some traditions slaughter or hunt animals to preserve their meat and fur during winter.

During Samhain, as during Beltane, the veil between realms gets thinner. This time of the year is related to the Underworld and ancestry work. It is a time to remember those who are no longer with us. It is also favorable for divination and other psychic abilities.

Places without the Four Seasons

The Wheel of the Year was developed with a European viewpoint, and it matches European seasonal cycles and agricultural changes. Because of this, it does not fit the natural rhythm of every place. If your goal is to connect with the changes in nature and honor its cycles, it's important that you do it locally; your celebrations and rituals should follow regional observations.

The four-season model also has a big flaw for some places of the earth: There are not four seasons. For example, in the tropics, the seasons are divided into wet and dry, and in the polar zones, there are only winter and summer.

You can craft your own wheel, one that matches your reality and focuses on the changes you feel and observe around you during the year. You can use the Wheel of the Year as inspiration, but I think the best option is to research local festivals because they probably already match your climate.

Climate Change

We as humans are facing a global threat: climate change. This disruption in the standard climate patterns has caused disturbances and modifications in the conventional seasons and climate regimens.[11] Because of it, some traditions don't match the current weather anymore.

It is a sad reality, but it should be taken into account when planning your rituals. For example, some rituals might ask for a white winter in places where it hardly ever snows now. Part of adapting your craft to the cycles surrounding you is to observe them and question whether traditional customs still fit them.

On a more personal note, I also think that we, as witches that work hand in hand with nature, should participate in helping minimize the harmful effects of climate change. The anthropogenic causes of global warming have been proven in many studies; we need to demand a new way to develop our civilization that is respectful of nature.

CREATE YOUR OWN WHEEL OF THE YEAR

Marian Green writes in *A Witch Alone*, "If some of the witches of today thought more about the actual workings of nature and less of book-bound, set knowledge, they would gain more power in their magicks, more joy in their celebrations, and a greater sense of unity with their ancestors and the ancient faith they aim to follow. [. . .] It is from that restrictive form of belief that most of them are trying to untangle themselves!"[35]

Working on your own Wheel of the Year can be a powerful tool for creating that freeing connection with nature. This activity is especially relevant for those practitioners whose seasons don't match the Wheel of the Year, but it can be equally empowering for the witches with the four seasons.

Make the Wheel Your Own

Start by selecting a timeframe that matches your seasons. Look up the beginning and end of climate cycles in your zone and determine whether they match a given date, such as the solstices and equinoxes.

Seasonal changes are a common point of celebration for many cultures. Find out the local festivals that have these changes in their roots because they will be one of the most accurate ways to celebrate the local climate.

Moon changes mark the harvest for many cultures. They can also be a powerful resource to incorporate into your wheel. Don't be afraid to add nonsolar festivals or festivals without a fixed date to your wheel.

Finally, your wheel should be an entirely personal way to celebrate the cycle of the year. Add any important date for you, even if it is not nature-related. For example, your birthday commemorates a year traveling around the sun; it is a remarkable day. You can also include local festivals with particular importance where you live, as they are days of high energy (see page 120).

Astronomical Cycles

Many cultures have looked at the sky and realized that some events repeat periodically. To understand them, they developed different systems of astrology and astronomy. Astronomy is the set of laws that explain the celestial cycles, and astrology is the discipline that studies the effects that astronomical events have on the Earth. Although knowledge about astronomy has merged into a single field, many branches of astrology have survived. The correspondences stated in this book originate from modern Western astrology.

The Emerald Tablet is often cited when explaining the influence of the stars over the Earth. This cryptic Hermetic text was seen as the foundation of alchemy, and in it, you can read: "That which is above is like to that which is below, and that which is below is like to/from that which is above." This verse evolved into the popular occult phrase "as above, so below."

This sentence states the relationship between our world and celestial events, and it highlights the geocentric point of view of astronomy. To understand how celestial events affect life on Earth, we interpret them from our perspective.

Time and distance perception in outer space differ greatly from humans'. Some celestial cycles can take many human lives to be completed. They aren't less important, but I wanted to focus on those that can have a bigger impact on our daily lives as we can experience their changes several times in our lifetimes.

The Moon

The moon has fascinated humanity for centuries, and it has a relevant place in the occult and the craft. Sarah Faith Gottesdiener, the author of *The Moon Book*, describes the moon as the world's celestial anchor, the mirror of the seasons, the power of the water, and the representation of our interior.[36]

The moon travels across the sky, experiencing cyclical changes that we name phases and the twelve zodiac signs. Because of its predictable and relatively quick energy changes, the moon has become a highly popular celestial body for magickal timing (see page 129).

The duration of a lunar cycle depends on the reference point used to measure it. Two of the most common ways are tropical months and synodic months. A tropical month is the time it takes the moon to pass twice through the same point of the sky (around twenty-seven days and eight hours). A synodic month, or lunation, is the time that it takes the moon to complete a cycle around the Earth (around twenty-nine days and thirteen hours); to make this more practical, the cycle is considered twenty-eight days long.

Moon Phases

Moon phases can bring a big advantage to working with lunar magick. They are seen with a holistic approach, as parts of a whole process that allows growth and achievement. You can also use them separately to match the energy of your spell. There are eight phases on the moon cycle, although they can be simplified into four.

CORRESPONDENCES FOR MOON PHASES

Moon Phase		Correspondences
New Moon	● New Moon	End and beginning. Resting from the previous work and deciding how to move forward. Introspection, shadow work, and divination.
Waxing Moon	◐ Waxing Crescent	Getting organized, creating a plan, tuning in with the initial motivation, boosting your courage.
	◐ First Quarter	Committing to goals, hard work, personal growth, self-improvement, attracting positive things to your life, creating charms.
	○ Waxing Gibbous	Constructive magick, improvement of situations, reviewing plans, vitality and energy.
Full Moon	○ Full Moon	Peak energy, results, psychic abilities, divination, boosting spells, glamours, dream work, abundance.
Waning Moon	○ Waning Gibbous	Releasing tension, regrouping, socializing, working on your mental health.
	◑ Last Quarter	Seeking balance, self-care, reviewing the lessons you have learned, improving aspects of you that you don't like.
	◑ Waning Crescent	Cleansing, getting closure, detoxifying.

Moon mapping is a great strategy for better tracking your work. It consists of keeping track of the lunar phases and their energy and how they relate to you.

Note: Keep in mind that even though the phases occur simultaneously for both hemispheres, the image of the moon is different. It offers an upside-down image for the opposite hemisphere.

THE DARK MOON

We call the last one to three days of the waning moon the dark moon, when the moon cannot be seen and the sky is in complete darkness. It is an intense period that highlights the void and shadows in ourselves, but also boosts creativity and healing. The dark moon opens a gate to the lower self and the Underworld, making it an opportunity to cast light onto hidden aspects of ourselves or our craft. It allows us to deal with painful feelings or events in a raw way. However, it also leads the way toward closing wounds.

The Tides

One of the most representative effects of the moon on the Earth is the tides. Many ancient civilizations observed the relationship between our satellite and the sea, but it wasn't until gravity theory that we were able to comprehend it. The moon and the sun "pull" the water from the Earth's surface, displacing it and making the sea levels rise and lower at different points of the planet, creating the tides.

This cycle of high tides and low tides occurs every twenty-four hours and fifty minutes, including two high tides and two low tides. The rotation of the Earth and the sun's gravity pull over it are influenced by the moon, which adds those extra fifty minutes. Because of this, tides don't happen at the same hour every day.

The water levels for the different tides are also affected by the moon and correlate to the moon phases. During the new and full moons, the sun and the moon "pull" in the same direction, making tides more intense. During the first and last quarters, the moon and the sun "pull" in perpendicular directions, and the water is distributed more uniformly.

The influence that tides have over earthly life is bigger than what we might think at first. Many marine or semi-marine animals have adapted to tides, but it doesn't stop there. Terrestrial vertebrates that evolved from animals in the intertidal zone still retain those adaptations. Darwin theorized that was the reason behind human menstruation lasting about the same as a moon cycle.

The connection between the moon and tides runs deep; they have a synergic relationship. If you work with water or sea magick, consider using the correspondences for the tides in combination with moon magick.[37] In this table, you will find the tides that better relate to each phase. Remember tides change every six and a half hours.

If you don't live at the shore, it can be difficult to connect with the tides because they happen at different hours around the world. Choose a water body that is close to your home for observing these changes.

MOON PHASES AND THE TIDES

Moon Phase	Tide	Event	Correspondences
Full Moon	High Tide	The water is at its highest level.	Divination, manifestation, strength
Waning Moon	Ebb Tide	The water level lowers over several hours.	Releasing, banishing, cleansing, letting go, removal
New Moon	Low Tide	The water is at its lowest level.	Setting new goals, introspection, shadow work
Waxing Moon	Flood Tide	The water level rises over several hours.	Growth, new beginnings, rising energy, learning, prosperity

The Cycle of Life

The Planets and the Signs

In astrology and, in particular, in astrology charts, most celestial bodies fall under the umbrella term "planet," even if technically speaking they are not planets. Each planet projects particular energy over the Earth, affecting events on a global scale. In this book, I will focus on the solar system planets, including Pluto.

Depending on the velocity of the planet and its distance from the Earth, it takes more or less time to complete a lap through all the zodiac signs. This speed difference also creates two apparent types of movement between the planets: direct and retrograde. When the Earth "passes" a planet in its orbit, it seems to move backward in our sky. That is called retrograde, and the energetic correspondences change.

THE PLANET CORRESPONDENCES: DIRECT AND RETROGRADE

As we interpret astrology from a geocentric point of view, the planets travel across a particular zone of the sky. This section is divided into the twelve zodiac signs, including their constellations. Depending on the section where the planet is at each moment, its energy gets modified by that zodiac sign. Because each planet takes a different amount of time to complete a lap, the time it spends in a sign is different from the time other planets spend.

The sun and the moon also enter zodiac signs periodically. The sun's transit time is approximately one month, and the moon's is about two to three days. You can use the energy of the zodiac signs combined with moon phases or the seasons.

The Cycle of Life

Mercury
Direct correspondences:
Safe travel, good communication, starting a new business, technology improvements
Retrograde correspondences:
Delays and cancellations, miscommunications, technology problems, self-reflection, finding what was lost

Venus
Direct correspondences:
Beauty, relationships, partnerships, love, cooperation, sensuality, creativity
Retrograde correspondences:
Problems in relationships, creative block, deep feelings coming to light, changes of perspective

Mars
Direct correspondences:
Strength, assertiveness, aggressiveness, courage, passion
Retrograde correspondences:
Feeling tired and irritated, plans moving slowly, hurtful words, friction

Jupiter
Direct correspondences:
Abundance, expansion, philosophy, education, freedom, generosity, justice
Retrograde correspondences:
Introspection, personal transformation, philosophical doubts

Saturn
Direct correspondences:
Consequences, discipline, restrictions, boundaries, sacrifice, perseverance
Retrograde correspondences:
Reflection, stronger consequences, nuanced truth, improvement

Uranus
Direct correspondences:
Change, future, intuition, inventions, discovery, individuality, eccentricity
Retrograde correspondences:
Unexpected changes, unpredictable events, revolutions, confidence

Neptune
Direct correspondences:
Hidden aspects, psychic abilities, divination, dream work, illusion
Retrograde correspondences:
Insecurities, deception, feeling unsure about decisions, seeking meaning, spiritual transformation

Pluto
Direct correspondences:
Death and rebirth, transformation, regeneration, destruction, triumph
Retrograde correspondences:
Facing deep fears, core transformations, the subconscious, letting go

ZODIAC CORRESPONDENCES

Zodiac Sign	Correspondences
Aries	When a celestial body is under Aries's energy, it becomes an area of life where you can behave with confidence and even boldness. Aries leads and competes with courage and spontaneity.
Taurus	Taurus influences celestial bodies in a stable and pragmatic way. Decisions and actions become more prudent and long-lasting, sometimes getting a bit too close to stubbornness. It is also known for its sensual energy.
Gemini	This sign encourages accepting the duality that appears in all aspects of our life. The areas affected by Gemini are explored with rationality but also curiosity.
Cancer	This sign encourages following your intuition and your emotions. Cancer generates a nurturing energy but also promotes your finding of your own safe space.
Leo	Leo brings excellence, creativity, and pride. Actions will be modified with its creativity and attract praise. Although Leo stands up and speaks for itself, the areas affected by this sign need some external approval.
Virgo	The areas affected by this sign become a well-oiled machine. Organization and perfectionism, but with a practical touch, are traits that become indispensable. Attention to detail is key.
Libra	Libra stabilizes the aspects that are affected by its energy. It has a balancing energy that tries to create an educated and respectful environment, working well with others and acting with elegance. However, white lies to keep the peace can become a problem later on.
Scorpio	Resilience and survival identify the energy of this sign. The aspects it affects can enter a cycle of destruction and regeneration and make you lose interest. However, passion is always reborn with even more strength.
Sagittarius	Sagittarius searches for a deeper meaning, and it is not afraid to walk unknown paths. Its influence generates confidence and calls for adventure without restrictions. Sometimes it needs to be balanced by slowing down and paying attention to details.
Capricorn	Capricorn's energy can feel solitary as it focuses on self-reliance. The areas affected act with pragmatism but usually follow traditions, some in an overly rigid way. Responsibility and structure make mundane topics make sense, particularly those related to the mundane world.
Aquarius	The areas affected by Aquarius reject social norms, but they still seek finding their own place in society. There is a particular way to understand and address issues, often in with an analytic and rational (and sometimes cold) perspective.
Pisces	Pisces expresses its influence with imagination and emotions. Some actions might seem unaligned with your immediate focus, but they serve a higher goal. Intuition and devotion appear frequently, but they can also lead to disappointment.

With the rise of the Internet, accessing this information has become increasingly easier. You can find reliable astrological charts and forecasts online to help you understand the celestial situation and the upcoming transits and changes. As with any other source, it is important to research that your source is trustworthy and follows the same branch/tradition as you.

Other Cycles

The cycles mentioned in this chapter aren't the only ones you will encounter in your life. Your body and your environment will go through repetitive phrases. Paying attention to the pace of things will help you get in tune with them and make the most of the energy they bring into your life.

Circadian rhythms are one of the most relevant cycles in our daily lives. They regulate the sleep–wake cycle, which is repeated approximately every twenty-four hours. It can be found in most beings exposed to night–day change because it allows our bodies to regulate their functions via the circadian clock, controlling hormones, digestion, sleep, body temperature, and other body functions.[38]

Although all individuals from a species share a similar circadian clock, the clock differs slightly from human to human because it can be affected by external influences (e.g., screen time, drugs, illnesses, bedtime, jet lag), mutations, and climate where you live. Working against your circadian rhythm can negatively affect your health.[39] Circadian rhythms also determine your level of energy throughout the day; the two usual divisions are early birds and night owls. It's not unusual for this to change depending on age or routine.

Adapting to your natural circadian clock can help you in your craft as you can adapt your practice to your energy levels. I prefer casting spells when my energy is high because some can feel draining; however, it is easier for me to contact the Otherworld in the afternoon when I'm a bit tired (but not too tired). I don't recommend doing magickal workings when your energy levels are low because your reaction capacity decreases.

Another cycle that has been traditionally linked to magick forces, for good and bad, is menstruation. Historically it has been seen as something powerful, but it has also been used to deem menstruating people, particularly women, as "unclean." Because of this, some movements have used it as an empowering symbol.

Menstruation has a strong link to the moon because its average cycle lasts the same amount of time as the lunar cycle, twenty-eight days. This is probably related to our marine ancestors and their relationships with the tides (see page 69). It is not clear whether there is a relationship between moon phases and menstrual phases; studies support both answers. The most recent studies suggest that there was a relationship, but modern lifestyle changes have disrupted it.[40] This might explain the origin of the word menstruation, which derives from the Greek word *mene*, or "moon." Bodies experience changes during the

menstrual cycle. Some people experience them in a stronger way than others. Learning to identify and understand these changes can help you synchronize your craft with them. For example, if you suffer from strong PMS, it might be better to schedule heavy emotional rituals for a different time.

The uses of menstrual blood have changed through history. This has been strongly intertwined with misogyny, and it was often used as a weapon against women to deem them as "polluted," especially in but not limited to Western cultures. Because of this, it became a taboo topic, and many traditions involving menstrual blood were transmitted orally and not documented.

Traditional uses for menstrual blood include love magick, fertility spells, hexes and curses, and binding spells. Modern witchcraft has incorporated new ways to use it in the craft, including healing, nurturing, growth, change, and self-love. As society changes its way of understanding menstruation, so does the craft.

CHAPTER 5

Upper-, Mid-, and Underworld

To be able to get in touch with the energy of our universe, we need to understand the relationships that exist among all its inhabitants. In many witchcraft branches, there is a belief that our universe is divided into different realms. This distinction between worlds explains the existence of forces and entities that affect our everyday lives.

—

Ancient rulers and
Xenial laws whirled
Into the Underworld.
Scrutinize time
Many eternities shine,
Under the bright lights
Nature restarts and thrives.
Differences unfurl
In the Upperworld.

—LIDIA PRADAS

—

These realms are interconnected and can affect each other. There are many explanations and models to describe how they are organized, their characteristics, and how they interrelate. Witches, as walkers of the liminal, are able to travel through the thresholds of the realms and interact with them, and understanding each realm is essential to safe practice. This chapter will explore the theory of the two realities, ours and the Otherworld, and the theory of three worlds, the Upperworld, the Midworld, and the Underworld.

Two Realities

To understand the realms, the first division that has to be defined is between the mundane world and the Otherworld.[31, 41] The mundane world is sometimes also called the physical world because it is made of what we can experience in our everyday life, our reality in the material world. The Otherworld encompasses all the other realms. It is inhabited by spirits, gods, ancestors, faeries, and other entities.

This division is a way to classify the two realities based on our human experience; it doesn't mean they can't interact. Some aspects of our reality are deeply intertwined with the Otherworld, including spirits of the land anchored to a particular landscape (see page 107). Similarly, the Otherworld can be experienced and explored by humans with the proper techniques and knowledge. Some of the most common ways to do so are inhibitory practices such as meditation, trance, and lucid dreaming. Some locations,

such as thresholds, are more prone to helping you connect with the Otherworld; these are usually called liminal places.[42]

The reasons to work with the Otherworld are many, and each practitioner has their own motivations. It is important to know that there are also dangers. Because of this, it is better to explore it slowly but surely, deeply researching each realm and always establishing a way to come back to the mundane world before you leave it.

In their books, Christopher Penczak and Mat Auryn describe the concept of reality maps.[3, 24] Reality maps are models created to help us understand realms in order to be able to work and travel within and between realities. However, because reality is subjective, reality maps can differ from one person to another.

The Three Worlds

In Celtic, Norse, and reconstructionist traditions, one of the principal ways to conceptualize the Otherworld is the three worlds division: Upperworld, Midworld, and Underworld. The Upperworld is inhabited by the gods, the Midworld by humans and faeries, and the Underworld by the dead.[3, 41, 31]

The Otherworld includes the Upperworld and the Underworld. The Midworld is shared by our reality and some realms of the Otherworld, such as faeries, genius loci, and other spirits. This division is not airtight; some deities reside in the

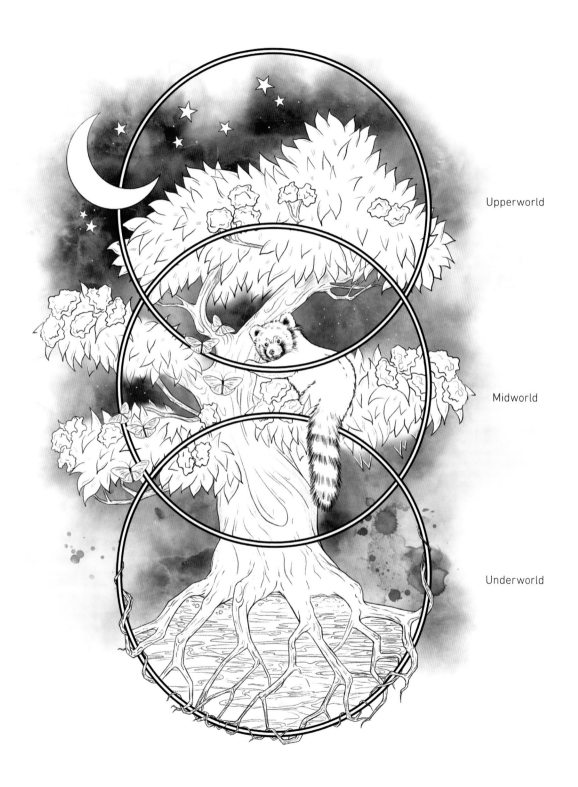

Upperworld

Midworld

Underworld

Underworld (for example, Hades or Hel), and the dead can be linked to the Midworld. Depending on the cultural background, these realms are connected by the tree of life, also known as *Yggdrasil* or *axis mundi*. This imagery of "world trees" or "trees of life" is present in the Ancient Greek, Norse Pagan, Incan, Mayan, and Ancient Egyptian religious systems.

The differences between how cultures conceptualize this division often become more noticeable as we dig deeper into the dynamics of the three worlds. In this book, we explore the modern reconstructionist view of them. The "gates" to each realm simply mean that the energy of the stated element is the closer match in mundane terms to the energy present in the Upper- and Underworld, respectively. Because of that, contacting the energy of these elements can be a help for traveling through the axis mundi to other realms.

The Upperworld

The Upperworld is the celestial realm, the heavens. It includes deities, planetary powers, and superior entities. It is an aerial, immaterial realm full of light. Time isn't linear; past, present, and future occur simultaneously.[31] It is often related to absolute knowledge, the ultimate wisdom, and divine consciousness.[3] The Air Gate is of the ways to access the Upperworld. Aidan Wachter describes it as "cold and void, un-human and removed." It is linked to the higher self (see page 37).

The Underworld

The Underworld is perceived as fluid and even warm because the Water Gate allows us to contact it.[41] It is the home of ancestors, death deities, animal powers, and other spirits. Intuition and the unconscious feed from it. It is where you can find the primal consciousness and the collective consciousness formed by the global ancestors.[3] In a sense, the Underworld is more familiar to us, a second home, because a part of our soul will merge with the rest of our ancestors there after our death. It is linked to the lower self (see page 37).

The Midworld

The Midworld is where humans live. It is our physical reality, made from the four elements—Air, Fire, Water, and Earth—and ruled by physical laws. It is as full of magick as the Upperworld and the Underworld, with its own energy, relationships, and entities (see page 107). It is linked to the middle self (see page 37).

Humans are not the only inhabitants of the Midworld; we share it with other entities that belong to the Otherworld. Aidan Watcher reflects on this in his book *The Six Ways*[41] and explains that these spirits are closer to us, and, at the same time, they are the most dangerous and helpful beings that you can encounter. This is because we share the same world; they can intervene with more intensity in our reality.

The Elements

The elements are the main components of our realm. They are the origin of all things. Although they shape the physical reality, they are present in both physical and unmanifested (or nonphysical) forms.[43] Their existence goes beyond physical terms. Their attributes transcend to different types of energy and magick.[44] As Christopher Penczak describes them, "The elements are immeasurable archetypal energies of creation. They can be felt and experienced, but not measured by our current scientific methods. Their names are symbolic for their nature."

It is difficult to find many things in our realm that show the elements' purest form. As the building blocks of the Midworld, they often appear mixed. To create types of energies or substances, each element needs to be present in a particular amount, and the quantity of each element creates the materials in our reality. If those "percentages" aren't correct, the imbalance will generate problems. In witchcraft, when you change the balance of something's elements, you transform it into a new substance.[45]

The understanding of the elements is to some extent culturally based. For example, the Celts believed in three elements (Fire, Earth, and Water), and Chinese tradition focuses on five elements (Wood, Fire, Earth, Metal, and Water). This doesn't mean there is one "right version" of them. They are simply different human-made classifications for the same natural fundamentals.

In this book, you will find information about the most widespread Western version of the elements: the four physical elements (Air, Fire, Water, and Earth) and the Spirit element, or quintessence. These elements were developed by ancient Greeks and refined by medieval alchemists, which resulted in the historical version of chemistry. However, if you want to work with the spirits of the land, my advice is to research traditional correspondences of the elements at the specific location (see page 107).

Some people might only see the elements as a way to organize magick, recognizing particular energies and their relationships.[44, 43] Other practitioners treat them almost as spirits or entities. A third view is of elemental realms: the pure state of the elements that intersect with reality and represent the core energy of the element.[45]

If we organized the four elements according to their closeness to the physical realm, Earth would be the closest one, then Water, then Fire, and finally Air. Some authors switch the positions of Fire and Air, but I prefer this classification because Fire does have a visual appearance while Air doesn't. The fifth element, also called quintessence, unites them all and belongs to the Otherworld.

It is important to note that the names we use for the elements are metaphorical, a way to interpret the nature of these energies. Mat Auryn describes them in this way: Earth is perceived as slow, stable, and dense energy.[3] Water is a relatively lighter, colder energy with a flowing quality. Fire is an unstable and fluctuating hot energy, and Air is warm and steady but flowing energy.

Understanding and Working with the Elements

The elements are raw powers with their own gifts and challenges. They are often represented as opposing and codependent forces, and working with them requires balance. All energetic "fingerprints" of substances can be simplified to combinations of the element. Understanding the "elemental recipe" that would bring about your desired outcome makes it easier to manifest it by tapping into these particular energies.

This might sound a bit overwhelming, but it doesn't need to be perfect. Once you have stripped your reality down to the bone, the true reality of the elements will be presented to you. The correspondences listed in the following sections, (as well as other books about the elements) are a good guide to help you figure out these combinations as you refine your practice and tune into the energies within you and around you.

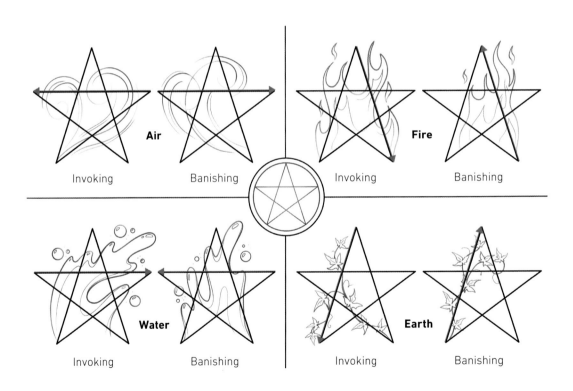

How to trace banishing and invoking pentagrams[3, 45]

EARTH CORRESPONDENCES

Rituals	Wealth, prosperity, fertility, stability, family, friendships, grounding
Ritual Forms	Burying, planting, making images in soil/sand
Season	Winter
Time	Night
Point of life	Advanced age
Sense	Touch
Symbols	Salt, clay, soil, rocks, plants, bones, colors brown and green

Table 1. Earth Correspondences. Modified from: *Earth, Air, Fire & Water: More Techniques of Natural Magic* by Scott Cunningham[43]

WATER CORRESPONDENCES

Rituals	Purification, nurturing, emotions, love, psychic awareness, dreams, sleep
Ritual Forms	Dilution, placing into water, washing away, bathing, sprinkling
Season	Autumn
Time	Dusk
Point of life	Maturity
Sense	Taste
Symbols	Shells, a cup of water, chalice, color blue

Table 2. Water Correspondences. Modified from: *Earth, Air, Fire & Water: More Techniques of Natural Magic* by Scott Cunningham[43]

Earth

Earth is the densest of the elements, the solid state of matter. It represents the most material aspect of our realm, and sometimes it is seen as the physical realm itself. It moves slowly, but it is committed to its causes. It is patient and experienced, rarely allowing external disturbances, but has punctual "violent ruptures," such as earthquakes, after enduring something for a long time.

The energy of this element is defined by abundance and fertility, stability and steadiness, growth and structure. Earth is considered a receptive element. It is the body and bones, the beginning and the end of the cycle. The Earth nourishes all life, and all life will go back to it when it dies.

Water

Water is the second densest element. It can be touched and held, but it doesn't have a shape. It is related to emotions and psychic abilities. Some practitioners tie it to the astral realm. It shares many parallels and ties with the moon. It is mutable, and it has phases or tides. Its energy is nurturing and adaptive, but it can also quickly become overwhelming and destructive, as with floods. It shows the power of transformation in its different states: steam, liquid water, and ice.

The energy of this element is defined by intuition and psychic abilities, emotions and dreams, healing and nurturing. Water is considered receptive energy. It is a protective womb, but it is simultaneously a cold place, the unknown subconscious.

FIRE CORRESPONDENCES

Rituals	Purification, destruction, passion, sexuality, force, anger, courage, banishing
Ritual Forms	Burning, melting, heating, baking
Season	Summer
Time	Noon
Point of life	Youth
Sense	Sight
Symbols	Flame, lava, candle, heated object, spicy food, color red

Table 3. Fire Correspondences. Modified from: *Earth, Air, Fire & Water: More Techniques of Natural Magic* by Scott Cunningham[43]

AIR CORRESPONDENCES

Rituals	Travel, learning, communication, freedom, knowledge, lost objects
Ritual Forms	Tossing objects into the air, sound, visualization, creating airflows, blowing
Season	Spring
Time	Dawn
Point of life	Infancy
Sense	Hearing, smell
Symbols	Feather, smoke, bells, color yellow

Table 4. Air Correspondences. Modified from: *Earth, Air, Fire & Water: More Techniques of Natural Magic* by Scott Cunningham[43]

Fire

Fire is closer to the spirit realm, representing energy in a pure form. The element of transmutation, our soul's sparkle, transforms empty beings into living beings. A flame constantly changes its shape, converting fuel into light and heat. The energy of this element is protective but also destructive. A fire can heat you during a cold night, but it can also burn your home down.

The energy of this element is defined by passion and courage, anger and intensity, joy and confidence. Fire is considered a projective element. It is the internal force that keeps us moving.

Air

Air is the closest element to the Otherworld. It is shapeless and invisible; we can feel it but not confine it. Because of this, it is related to intangible concepts, ruling the realms of thoughts, mind, knowledge, and memory. It is a steady force, but it is not grounded. Just as the wind shapes stones, it has the will-power to create profound changes with slow action, but then the sand is carried away, reaching and exploring new places.

The energy of this element is defined by knowledge and memory, language and communication, movement and intel-ligence. Air is considered a projective element. If Water is the subconscious, Air is our consciousness, what we do deliberately.

Quintessence

The quintessence (or spirit, in some witchcraft branches) is the element that belongs to the Otherworld. It is the energy that keeps the other elements together and allows them to create our reality. It is part of the four elements and contains them simultaneously.[3] It's like the spider web, which is made from spider silk and at the same time keeps the spider silk together.

The quintessence is pure, raw energy that creates balanced patterns with unlimited potential. The energy of this element is associated with our higher self, deities, entities, the Otherworld, and astral traveling. Spirit is considered both a projective element and a receptive element.

Elemental Relationships

The existence of the elements as individual forces is important—as are the relationships between them.[46] Together they make possible our reality. The polarity of receptive/projective leads to oppositions, and this in turn leads to imbalances. Air and Earth are seen as opposites, and so are Water and Fire.

When an imbalance occurs, the properties of an element are exacerbated and generate a negative impact. To fix or prevent this, we use rituals related to the opposite element, balancing their energies.

Note: Some symptoms can also be a sign of an illness. If they present strong or repeatedly, ask a health professional.

ELEMENTAL IMBALANCES

Element	Imbalance Effects	Balancing Activities
Air	Losing touch with reality and the connection with the mundane or physical world	Earth activities: grounding, mindfulness, nature-related hobbies
Fire	Explosive emotions or dangerous emotions, such as extreme anger or aggression	Water activities: journaling about emotions, meditation, intuition work, swimming, baths
Water	Drowning in emotions, passiveness, apathy, not being able to express it	Fire activities: exercise, adventures, emotional media, self-expression activities, socializing
Earth	Pessimism, stubbornness, cynicism, shooting down dreams without trying	Air activities: making crafts, creative activities, fantasy media, philosophical discussions

Table 5. Elemental Imbalances. Modified from *The Path of the Witch*.[21]

The relationship between and balance of the five elements are represented with a pentacle. This symbol represents the connection and interdependence of the five elements while also showing each of them as a whole.

The pentacle is used as the invoking and banishing symbol for the elements, depending on the direction and the beginning point where it is traced. There are slight differences surrounding how to do this, particularly when it comes to Water and Air. The illustration on page 82 shows show one of the most common versions I use. Another way to invoke and dismiss the elements is by using symbols that represent them and calling the elements into them for the spell's duration.

Mundane Knowledge

Mundane derives from the Latin *mundus*, meaning "world." Mundane knowledge is that earthly wisdom in touch with our surroundings and our present—the knowledge of our reality in the Midworld. Sometimes it is seen as trivial or superficial compared to our concept of witchcraft as esoteric wisdom, mysteries of the occult hidden from outsiders. The truth is that they are two sides of the same coin. Without the mundane, magick wouldn't exist. I differentiate between three main types of mundane knowledge, but they are not the only ones: history and folklore, environment, and safety.

History and Folklore

Understanding the origins of your practices and the conditions in which they initially developed will help you gain a better understanding of them. We can misinterpret a lot of things if we don't have context. One of the most common examples is the use of "eyes of newt" in potions when, in context, what it meant was mustard seeds.

Folklore is very important, particularly local folklore. As knowledge and traditions are globalized, some grow popular while others are forgotten. If you intend to work in a specific location, familiarize yourself with the entities found there, their preferences, and their habits (see page pages 104–107).

Environment

You need to know how nature works if you want to connect with it. Research the local ecosystems where you live and the species that inhabit them. Learn about their natural cycles, the benefits they provide to our lives, and the dangers they pose.

It's also fascinating to read about how people who have lived in the area for centuries use indigenous flora and their relationships with them. For example, in places where heliotrope was common, it was said to repel witches, while in areas where it was rare, it was considered a sign of their presence.

Learn how to recognize local plants and animals (or their tracks), and you will be more aware of the life that surrounds you. You'll notice that your connection to nature grows stronger!

Safety

Understanding the laws that rule the physical world can prevent disappointments, accidents, and even more significant damage. Some things that you should be aware of:

- Some herbs and crystals are highly toxic.

- Not all ingredients that are safe for humans are safe for pets and vice versa.

- Herbal remedies can interact with medications.

- Animal remains can carry diseases and should always be disinfected if you find them in the wild.

- Some stones, minerals, and metals can create chemical reactions when exposed to certain types of liquids.

- Small crystals in jar candles can explode because of the heat.

- Essential oils are not made for internal use.

- Some witchy shops sell herbal mixes without saying what's inside, putting people with allergies in danger.

- Cauldrons get hot and should be kept on heat-resistant surfaces.

It is imperative to research toxicity, fire safety, the chemical composition of crystals, and other safety concerns before using any tool.

Upper-, Mid-, and Underworld

The Six Ways

The Six Ways is a representation of our reality.[41] This three-dimension map depicts the three worlds and the four elements. It can be found in different ceremonial and traditional magick branches under other names.

As is the witch's hexagram (see page 32), it is drawn as three lines or double-pointed arrows of the same length, crossed in the middle.[23] The central arrow should point up and down in a three-dimensional representation, while the other two are in the same plane.

We can divide the six ways into three levels: up where the Upperworld is; middle where you can find the Midworld divided into the four directions; and down, the Underworld.

Each one of these corresponds to a point of the diagram, and the directions are associated with their correspondent elements:

- Up: the Upperworld
- Down: the Underworld
- Crosspoint: the Midworld
- North: Earth
- East: Air
- South: Fire
- West: Water[41]

Upperworld

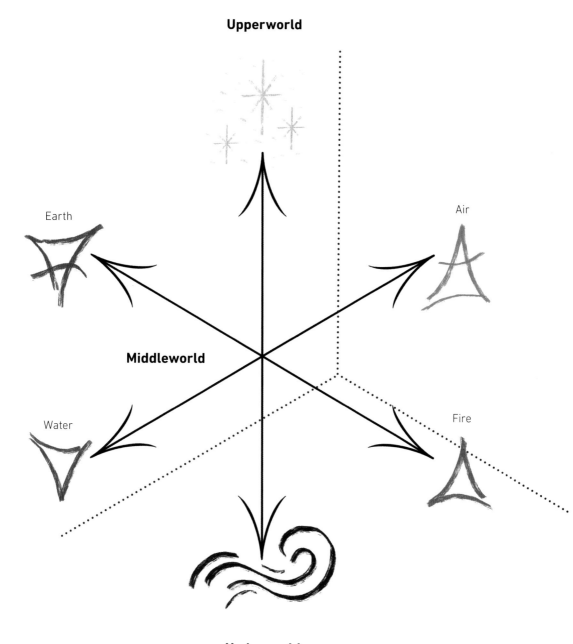

Earth

Air

Middleworld

Water

Fire

Underworld

TRAVELING THE AXIS MUNDI

Traveling to other realms falls under the name flying. Flying consists of abandoning your body, the physical part of yourself that links you to the Midworld, and exploring other realms. Different techniques—such as lucid dreaming, astral traveling, breath control, and trance—permit this division. They are classified as out-of-body experiences, or OBE. Some witches also use compounds, or entheogens, that help during the process, but they should always be taken with caution and under the supervision of an expert. Your health is a priority and should not be put at risk during an OBE.

Crossing the Hedge

The separation between your body and consciousness can create vulnerabilities because not all spirits have good intentions. Cleanse yourself, create a protective barrier, and adventure in a calm state of mind.

Once your mind is in a liminal state, visualize the axis mundi. It is often depicted as a giant tree with deep roots that go to the profundities of the Underworld and strong branches that spread over the Upperworld. You should be near the base of the trunk.

Note: Before doing the next step, some practitioners, particularly beginners, like to create a bond, like tying a string to that moment and place, to come back more easily by just following the energy link or "safe line." Focus on the present moment and transform that energy into the fingerprint of your energy link. Visualize a golden rope attached to the chest of your physical body and to your soul. Then knot it to the tree. The rope is infinite and unbreakable. You might not always see it while you are exploring, but it will be there every time you reach for it.

Touch the sacred tree of realms and feel its energy, the energy that connects everything in this realm and others, in this time and others. Get in sync with it, allow it to flow through you, and merge with it. Now, you should be able to travel through the bridge between worlds.

Once you have created that energetic connection, focus on exploring the axis tree. Feel how its roots dig into the dense energy of the Underworld and how its branches expand in the ethereal atmosphere of the Upperworld. The same way that sap travels through trees, allow your energy to merge with the flow of the axis tree and transport you to the desired realm.

When you want to go back, make your way back to the tree using your safety line if needed. Hop into the energy flow and follow the line until you reach our reality and are back to your body. Recover your conscious slowly, and focus on recognizing your surroundings. Ground yourself to recover your full presence.

The reasons to travel to the Otherworld are many. One of the most common is searching for knowledge or advice from the experiences and entities that inhabit it. You can also find healing through answers, energy, or interactions along your journeys. Finally, another typical reason is to establish contact with some entities: You can talk with them, create bonds, ask for help, or even create pacts.

Safety in Other Realms

Any time we visit the Otherworld, there are rules that we should observe if we want to prevent possible future problems.

- Stay close to the axis mundi, particularly if it is a zone that you haven't explored in the past. Even if you have a safe line, it is better to be able to come back to our realm fast if something goes wrong.

- Be polite. This is the main rule for all your interactions in the Otherworld. Don't insult entities, respect their possessions, don't provoke them, and ask for permission. However, some of their social conventions might not be similar to ours. That's why you need to know the kind of entity you interact with.

- Don't eat, drink, or exchange bodily fluids. It can be considered a pact by many entities.[32]

- Trust your intuition. If you feel that something is off, don't be afraid to set and enforce boundaries. Close contact and come back to our realm if you think it is necessary.

- Carry talismans with you. Keep an amulet or a crystal with you for protection.

Apart from these steps, there are other things you should do in the mundane realm for a safer experience. Keep your mind, body, and soul aligned and protected. It is advisable to work on your shadow self, understand yourself better, and create an energy shield. Protect the place where you experience OBE, as well as your home, to avoid the entrance of unwanted presences.

—

**Any time we visit the Otherworld,
there are rules that we should
observe if we want to prevent
possible future problems.**

—

CHAPTER 6

LAND WITCHCRAFT

As mentioned in chapter 2, after exploring the world inside you, the next step is to explore the outside world. And now that we understand the importance of the rhythm of the universe and the different realms in our reality, we can dive into how they merge. The earth is full of magick and mysticism, and this chapter focuses on the power of the mundane world. It is an area often looked down on by some parts of the spiritual community, but the magick of nature is a direct branch of the magickal arts, derived from many years of accumulated knowledge around the globe, that taps on the limitless powers of nature.[44]

—

Take a walk at night. Walk so silently that
the bottoms of your feet become ears.

—SONIC MEDITATION,
PAULINE OLIVEROS

—

The divine within nature is a topic that has fascinated all cultures. We see signs of this in sacred places of high energy, in the ancient depictions of landscapes, and in mythologies and folklore. It is in the mountains, rivers, and all of the natural elements of a place. The ecosystems profoundly influence the spirits you can find in a place, the natural elements you can use, and even the culture that developed and is developing there.

The secrecy of some witchcraft traditions promotes isolation and keeping your craft to yourself, thus indoors. And it is easy to fall into solitude and become disconnected from the outside and the natural world. Deepening our knowledge and our connection with our local natural environment is one of the best ways to reconnect with our power.

The Difficult Relationship between Humans and Nature

The relationship that humans have with nature is complex. The Industrial Revolution is often seen as a turning point at which the pact between people and earth was broken. However, new research shows it isn't that simple. Humans evolved in Africa, and the African (and some European) ecosystems evolved with us. When humans started spreading 22,000 years ago to different parts of the planet, they encountered naive fauna that had never met a human hunter, especially in America and Australia.[47, 48]

Megafauna—large-size animals, such as bison, buffalo, bears, horses, deer, and extinct animals such as giant sloths or mammoths—suffered the most. Their populations had already started to decline, but the systematic killing in small numbers of young individuals was enough to drive them to extinction.[49] This event is known as the overkill theory.[47, 50]

Without megafauna, ecosystems all around the globe changed, and humans did too. With the rise of extensive livestock and agriculture, some of the grazing and grasslands previously maintained by megafauna survived. This megafauna disappearance means that when we think about the balance between nature and humans before the Industrial Revolution, we only see what was left after an anthropogenic mass extinction of animals and the plants that depended on them. The overkill theory does not disregard that many human cultures reached an equilibrium with nature after the disappearance of megafauna and that this balance was disturbed by colonization and the Industrial Revolution.

Throughout the history of life on Earth, there have been five mass extinctions, meaning more than half of species disappeared in a relatively short period of time. The sixth mass extinction is the quick extinction of species that has been ongoing since the Holocene to this day, and that has been heavily influenced by human actions. In this context of unbalanced ecosystems, it is estimated that up to 150 species are lost every day because of human actions.[51]

This is not meant to dismiss the damage done to nature after the Industrial Revolution, nor the more sustainable ways that many cultures developed in the past around the globe. It is a call to action. Why are we trying to preserve the effects of extinction instead of trying to fix them?

Learning about the environment is important for witches. We need to understand that we are as much a part of nature as animals, plants, and stones are. We are part of the physical and spiritual web that links everything. We also need to keep in mind that every act has a consequence, good or bad. Our actions create changes. If we want to tap into the earth's energy, we need to restore the function that humans had and heal it as a whole, restoring the symbiotic energy between ecosystems and magick. It is our responsibility to study the natural and spiritual realms to at least try predict the results of our behavior.

The Environment and Witches

One of the most common representations of witches in the popular imagination is the wise woman in a small cabin in the woods living in communion with nature and its spirits. This idea stems from an idealized past, but there is some truth to it.

One of the most influential works on this view of witches is the book *La Sorcière* by the French historian Jules Michelet. In it, he offers a view of witches as both rebels and victims of the Christian Church, peasants oppressed by the ruling class and religions who found their liberation in ancient knowledge and living alone in natural

places. The concept of witchcraft emerged with the expansion of Christianity; their core beliefs go against the worship of pagan idols. However, with the publication of *De civitate Dei contra paganos* (or *On the City of God Against the Pagans*) by Augustine of Hippo in 426 BCE, it was made official for the church that all magick powers proceeded from demonic pacts.

This complete demonization of the craft led to a movement to eradicate the magickal practices of *sortilegium* and *maleficium*— sorcery and curses, magickal/pagan practices that they believed were inspired by the devil. This culminated in the Middle Ages with the spread of witch trials and the publication of *Malleus Maleficarum* (or *Hammer of Witches*) in 1486 BCE by the inquisitor Heinrich Kramer.

This was mainly aimed at the main pillars of herbal/medicinal knowledge and self-sustainability. But, "punishable witchcraft" is a concept created by humans, and they could tailor it to fit attitudes deemed undesirable by them.[52] Nature was seen as dirty and chaotic, something that should be tamed and serve the children of God. Understanding nature in this way underscored the relationship between witches and the natural world.

More often than not, the victims of witch persecution were just regular people, but sometimes there were other motivations behind it. Some were seen as undesirable because their actions could threaten the established order:

- A person who could use natural remedies to cure ailments went against the idea of illness and disease being a punishment or a test from God.

- Herbal preparations that allowed women to plan pregnancies, understand their sexology, and control menstrual cycles went against the idea of having as many kids as God sent.

- Living away from towns and possessing knowledge about foraging and self-sufficiency was a threat to feudal lords.

- Widows, literate people (especially women), people with disabilities, and people with attitudes those in power didn't like were dangerous because of their knowledge, their freedom, or simply their existence.[52, 53]

People persecuted and punished for witchcraft were not witches but people who made the rest of the community, the leaders, or the church uncomfortable with their behavior or knowledge.

Heal Your Relationship with the Land
As Scott Cunningham wrote in his book *Earth Power: Techniques of Natural Magic*, the magic of nature is uncomplicated and direct, derived from the people's experimentation before us around the globe.[44] The mystery of natural magick is there are no mysteries.

If you need to restore your spiritual connection with nature, you need to experiment with it yourself. It is not enough to know about it; you need to be conscious of it.[54] You might have passed near the same tree a hundred times, but have you stopped to observe it? To really know that tree? Touch its bark, follow its changes through the seasons, observe the animals that enjoy it, feel its energy, and feel how it connects with the rest of the elements of nature.

Experiment with your surroundings like a child. Rediscover them with excitement by paying attention to each detail. Learn about cycles and relationships in nature and how a small change can affect nature's web. Discover the spirits linked to that space.

One of the main reasons people feel disconnected from the land is that they don't have direct access to (quiet) natural spaces. The urban way of living has concentrated civilization into specific spots and created a barrier between human customs and nature. If you're in this situation, you might have to travel to find a natural space. As this takes time, plan your trips ahead. Make a list of what you want to study and experiment with, making the most of your time in nature.

Another great way to heal your connection with nature is by helping it to recover through partaking in activities meant to protect it. This can be small changes in your daily life, or it may mean joining global movements. Your path will come naturally to you because once you create an emotional bond with the land and your surroundings, you will want to protect it.

BONDING WITH NATURE

The Taoist author Mantak Chia presents trees as entities with stable energy that can absorb negative energy and transform it into more positive energy. Who hasn't felt calm and rejuvenated after spending time outdoors? This modified version of his exercise for befriending a tree is one of my favorite ways to reconnect with the land.

This exercise focuses on using your hands to create a connection. As we saw in the exercise Receiving and Projecting Energy (see page 12), the hands are especially sensitive for energy interchange. This exercise deepens the method by controlling your own energy and using your hands to create a connection. You will be interacting with the inner energy of another living being.

Befriend a Tree

First, find a healthy tree that you feel drawn to, preferably a big and old tree because its links with Mother Earth and Time will be more robust. Get familiar with its shape, texture, species, smell, and characteristics. I find it easier to do this with a tree that I often encounter in my daily life.

Present yourself to it and ask for its permission to work with its energy. Pay attention carefully to the energy that it emanates, and if it is receptive, place your two palms over it.

Close your eyes and connect your energy with the tree's. Feel yourself merge with it and with the rest of the landscape. Become part of the energy circuit that flows through the tree.

When you are ready, disconnect from the tree's energy gently and separate your hands. Thank the tree before going away.

Once you have created a relationship with a tree, it will be easier to reconnect with it from time to time and feel the different energy during the seasons. For example, if it is deciduous tree, it will have a weaker energy during winter. This practice is also a good way to explore new lands and establish a connection with a new place.

Unaligned Knowledge and Practices

It is easy to focus on world matters in a globalized world, leaving aside the local aspect of your craft. Connecting with your nearest environment is the way to reconnect with your power. In ecological movements, this approach is often known as bioregionalism: the concept that only the small scale is sustainable.

To achieve this, we need to unlearn some things. Much of the mainstream information about witchcraft available nowadays focuses on Western culture and Anglo-Saxon influence in particular. You must ask yourself: Does this serve its purpose in my circumstances?

When I talk about reconnecting with the land, one of the first things I recommend is learning about the ecology of the place where you live. Some witches celebrate seasonal festivals that don't match their seasons, looking for plants that don't grow where they live, working with spirits that don't inhabit their land. Through conscious knowledge of your surroundings, you will be able to predict its reactions to your magick more accurately.

This is also a realistic approach to the amount of knowledge that you can reasonably acquire in a lifetime. You cannot memorize all the landscapes in the world— but you can become an expert on the nature around you and develop a true bond with it. By reducing the scale, you can experiment with things that otherwise would have gone unnoticed. Familiarizing with your surroundings will open new opportunities for you to find local ingredients, entities, and traditions. It is an effective way to connect with the land and empower your magick, and it is also a way to simplify your craft.

Studying Your Surroundings

As we have seen, magick has rules, and it is not indifferent to the physical world. Knowledge of these rules is a must: You'll need it so that you can practice your magick well, become better at your craft, and more accurately predict the outcome of its use.

To acquire this knowledge, you need to step out of the occult-related books and turn to more mundane resources that are all around you. Some main pillars will allow you to deepen your understanding of your natural surroundings:

- Understand climate cycles in your area. Temperature, precipitation, and seasons limit the species that can be found and shape their behaviors. Climate influences and filters the types of life that can be supported by the land on a large scale.

- Learn to identify native plants, animals, and other organisms and their relationships. The "alive" part of a place is one of the most representative pieces of it. Sometimes this is thought of as a passive element, and that interactions only occur where the conditions are right; but species also actively change the conditions of their ecosystem— beavers and dams, for example.

- Learn the topography, geology, and type of soil of local ecosystems. This is the second big filter after climate. The land is molded with the earth's raw material, eroded by water, wind, and living beings. This is the foundation of an ecosystem and can allow it to thrive or not.

- Research the external influences that affect your local land. Sadly, this is an important variable that we have to take into account. When we find something that makes little sense, we need to ask ourselves the origin of that influence (e.g., human activity, accidents) and identify which natural process or element it is modifying. For example, when we see cigarette butts in the nests of birds near picnic places, we know they came from humans. The birds choose the soft material of the filters for their nests, but this also exposes them to toxins.

BIOREGIONALISM

Bioregionalism is a way to explore, study, understand, and protect nature and humans from a close-up point of view. Bioregions are defined by the relationship between their inhabitants, the climate, and the landscape. Bioregionalism highlights the unique ecology of each bioregion and helps us understand it.

The key to really understanding an ecosystem is thinking about it as a web. Ask yourself: If you touch a node, where will the threads transmit the vibration? This isn't easy to predict, and scientists are still investigating it, but there are well-established relationships that you can learn about.

Academic resources are useful, but another vital and essential aspect is first-hand observation. Experimenting with the outdoors is one of the easiest and fastest ways to learn about it. Active observation can be as straightforward or as complex as you want it to be. It can be limited to observing some of the seasons' changes or amplified to study even the smallest detail in nature.

The essential tools for a naturalist are the senses. An excellent step toward practicing active observation is getting yourself a field notebook and going outside. Take notes on what you see, feel, hear, and sense. Contrast that information with the books that you have at home.

The mundane world around you isn't the only thing that you should learn about. As you work with the land and local folklore, you will realize that it is full of spirits and entities linked to its nature and history. Josephine McCarthy, in her book *Magic of the North Gate*, establishes two approaches to magickally exploring the world around you: The first is through the religious and cultural frames of the place. The second is *without* the religious and cultural frames, exploring the powers directly.[13]

Both approaches can give you important information and be complementary. However, depending on your craft, one may be more suitable than the other. My personal advice is to first learn from the knowledge about local folklore gathered by people who came before you.

Adapting You Magick

As you learn to listen to your surroundings, you will start finding the dissonances between them and your craft. It can be a difficult process. Leaving a structured belief system for uncertainty and self-exploration can be scary. Sometimes it reaches a point when you need to decide whether to keep doing what is comfortable or take a leap and do what feels right.

At this turning point, it is not unusual to face a dilemma with certain practices that are dear to you, that you hold close to your heart, but that you now realize don't make sense in your context. At this point, I think the decision should be based on the question, *Does it serve a strong purpose in my craft?*

Allow yourself to be creative and flexible, exploring practices outside the mainstream ones. Cunningham says that three requirements must be present to perform effective magick: the need, the emotion, and the knowledge.[44] Take a leap and investigate outside the well-known practices to find those that suit your needs. Once you narrow your practice, you will realize that it is easier to discover details and patterns useful for your craft. This is the beginning to discovering your own magickal truth.[13]

Local Resources

As you start understanding and working with the land, focus on what you can find and also on how it can be incorporated into your craft.[35] Adapt your craft to what's available where you live; study and find uses for what is available around you. If you live in a tropical area and are trying to connect with the land, it makes little sense to use desert plants in your craft. It is plausible that a plant with similar characteristics grows in your zone, but it can take time, effort, and research to discover it.

Local plants, stones, and other natural resources are infused with the energy of local spirits; they are connected to you simply due to proximity.[31] If you start using plants that belong to the same place, you will realize how they create synergies between them, creating your own ecosystem of magick. In addition to the natural resources you can find in a place, there are intangible resources: folklore, customs, and oral knowledge. They help you understand the dynamics of your surroundings through the experiences and imaginations of the inhabitants who came before you.

Local Folklore

In the same way that you don't need to study the ecology of a place from scratch, you don't have to investigate its energy and spirits from point zero. Folklore is a precious source when it comes to learning about the spirituality of a place. You will be learning from the people who experienced it before you.[55] You may be lucky and find detailed books about local folklore and customs. In addition to those resources, one of the most enlightening experiences can come from simply talking with the people who live there, particularly the elders. Old legends and traditions are dying in some places; soak up all the knowledge while you can and write it down for future generations.

The information you can get from your surroundings' folklore is not limited to the legends and beliefs a culture has retained over time. Another great way to learn about the energies that reign in a place is to study the etymology of their name. In many cultures, places were named after a remarkable aspect of the sites, which was often related to their spirituality.

Legends are not a matter of the past. Entities such as chupacabra and Teke-Teke signify that folklore is still alive and compiling the energy that surrounds certain places or events. The emergence of relatively new stories revolving around spirits and other entities that last in time signifies that they are present and relevant in modern times.

Local Correspondences

There are many books about the correspondences of different items and their uses in the craft. However, correspondences tend to change across cultures because of the historical background of their uses and because each culture has developed different folklore and belief systems.

Begin by researching your tradition's culture. Keep in mind that not all natural resources have been studied and documented according to their uses in the craft, and sometimes they just don't fit your personal experiences. If that's the case, you can experiment and establish them yourself.

Kelden, an author who writes about traditional witchcraft, describes four ways to determine these correspondences yourself in *The Crooked Path*:

Folklore: Studying ancient peoples' uses for something or its appearances in legends and mythology can guide you toward its traditional correspondences. For example, Greek oracles were said to chew basil to promote their visions. Thus basil is usually linked to psychic abilities.

Physical appearance: Energies usually permeate the shape of natural elements. For example, big, round, yellow flowers are typically related to solar energy.

Effects on the human body: The reaction of our body can be a strong indicator of something's properties. For example, poisonous plants are typically used in harmful spells.

Asking the land spirits: If you have built a good relationship with the spirits that live in the land where something was found, you can ask them directly.[31]

Harvesting and Foraging

There are rules that you should remember when foraging natural items:

- Do as little damage to plants as you can. Use the adequate tools. Don't pull the whole plant from the soil.

- Research endangered species and do not damage them.

- Never harvest more than you need. Leave enough for the plant to recover and for the species that depend on that plant.

- Do not use foraged things if you aren't sure of what they are.

- Remember that stones can be houses or hiding places for some animals.

- Make sure to sanitize animal remnants before using them in your craft.

Always review your local laws and customs when foraging because some places have rules or beliefs against foraging. Regarding the use of animal remnants in the craft, there are divided opinions about it. Some witches see it as a way to honor the animal, while others see it as disrespectful. My advice is that if you want to use them, only use those that have been gathered ethically, and always be respectful with them.

Local Spirits

Once you have learned about the nature that surrounds you, you can move on into the realm of spirits. I advise exploring in this order because spirits are often linked to the physical realm and its characteristics. Once you know the physical realm, it's the moment to ask yourself, *What power inhabits here?*

It is vital to understand that spirits, faeries, deities, and other entities are real and powerful even if they don't have a corporeal form. Their realm isn't ours, but it doesn't mean that they can't affect the terrestrial world. Some links and doors allow us to contact and interact with each other. To learn more about spirits and other entities, see chapter 7.

Genius loci

A genius loci (plural *genii locorum*) is the spirit that protects a particular place. These spirits are usually connected to mainland features such as lakes, forests, or mountains. They are the representation of the physical surroundings of a place, and they are its essence. They belong to the Otherworld but the inhabit the Midworld.

CREATING A BOND WITH LOCAL SPIRITS
Here are some ways to show your appreciation to genii locorum and other spirits of
the land:

- Develop an emotional bond with the land.
  This kind of spirit knows if you appreciate
  their home the same way they do.

- Engage in proactive initiatives to protect
  the land. As you belong to this realm,
  you're able to do great things to protect it.

- Create an altar. Some spirits see shrines
  as homes or places to rests. Please do
  your research about what that spirit likes
  before you start working on it.

- Leave offerings. Ensure that the spirits
  like what you offer and that the offerings
  have been gathered in an ethical/ecolog-
  ical way.

- Communicate with them through methods
  such as automatic writing or drawing.

- Be honest and consistent with your
  approach. Most spirits will appreciate
  your efforts.[31, 55]

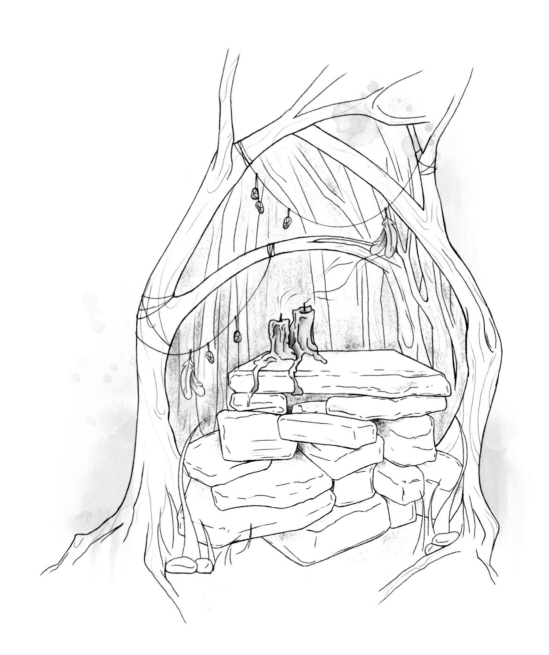

Land spirits are usually represented in a zoomorphic form, which allow them to move and interact with more freedom. But they can hide in many other shapes, as plants or mushrooms, nonliving things such as rocks or water, or even more legend-like forms as shadows. The main thing these forms have in common in that they always belong to the local landscape, and they never look out of place; although their energy might make them look special, such the enchanted wolves and bears in legends, or when you go on a hike and find a tree that seems to stand out from the rest.

Genii locorum are known for being protective of their spaces. The core of their existence is linked to the space. It is not unusual to find legends in which the protagonist gets punished for damaging their sacred places. With the record that humanity has of harming our environment, it shouldn't surprise us that they act cautiously or even have hostility toward us. Gaining the trust of a genius loci takes time; you need to create a bond with them and the land where they belong.

Other Entities

Genii locorum aren't the only entities with strong bonds to the land. From ghosts to faeries or even deities, many other beings are linked to a particular place.[56] Some places are more likely to attract spirits because they have a unique energy that allows them to act as links between realms. Judika Illes mentions the following in *Encyclopedia of Spirits*:

- Natural portals to their realms, such as wells, caves, and springs

- Natural thresholds, such as shores and mountain peaks

- Human-made thresholds, such as doorsteps and arches

- Thresholds between realms, such as cemeteries, birthing rooms, and ruins

- Sacred animals and plants

- Crossroads

- Traditional fairs, markets, and festivals

- Reflective surfaces and divination devices

- Shrines built where a spirit is known to inhabit[57]

Locating a spirit depends on the type of spirit, their story, and their powers. Learning about them and their legends will help you find the best places to encounter them.

CHAPTER 7

THE DEAD, THE SPIRITS, AND THE GODS

Working with the dead, spirits, or the gods means contacting the Otherworld. There are two approaches to this: calling entities into this realm or venturing into the liminal and their realms. Although both take practice, the second option is seen as a more advanced technique and should be practiced with caution.

—

I cannot prove to you that God exists, but my work has proved empirically that the pattern of God exists in every man and that this pattern in the individual has at its disposal the greatest transforming energies of which life is capable. Find this pattern in your own individual self and life is transformed.

—CARL JUNG, in a letter to Laurens van der Post

—

As you enter into this form of interaction, it is important to remember that these entities don't all follow the same set of rules. This may be all the truer if they belong to other realms. All entities have their differences, and they should not be treated in the same way. There are also differences between individuals; research has particular relevance and safety implications when working with them.

The first sections of this chapter will explore techniques that can be performed in the mundane world, and the last one will explain how to travel through realms. Not everyone wants to explore the liminal and Otherworld, and that's okay. Choosing not to is not an impediment to your craft. There are other ways to contact entities from our reality. The Midworld and the mundane reality have magick of their own, and many techniques don't require exploring other realms.

The Dead

The dead is a broad term encompassing different types of entities residing in the Underworld. It often includes the concept of ghosts, too, although they technically belong to the Midworld. The common denominator for them all is that, at some point, they were living beings residing in the Midworld, but they aren't anymore.

In *Magic of the North Gate*, McCarthy explains, "Not every person who dies goes straight onto the path of deep death to emerge into another life. Some stay around the living, some sink deep into the land to wait, and some, depending upon culture, stay within the land to act as an interface with the living."[13] In the craft, it is not unusual to work with the dead, ask them for advice, honor them, and get inspired by them. This can sound strange or even frightening for some people, but who hasn't brought flowers to the tomb of a loved one? Or kept a memento from them? Or even talked to them or felt their presence at some point? That's working with the dead.

One of the most common ways to interact with the dead is connecting with our ancestors. This feels easy because, in a way, they are the closest entity to us in the Otherworld. We are linked to them through our personal history, and we find comfort in them. Aidan Wachter explains, "We are all here due to the dead who came before us."[41] But our ancestors are not the only dead who can visit us. It is not unusual for people with experience to receive messages intended for other people. Sometimes the dead see in us an opportunity to communicate with others. There are two other classifications for the dead that are worthy of mention here: The forgotten dead are those spirits whose mundane life and name have been entirely forgotten by the living. The mighty dead are spirits whose exceptional actions in their lifetimes made them leave a positive and outstanding imprint on history.

A word about ghosts: They are middle selves or the cauldron of motion (see page 22) that couldn't return to the land after the death of the body they inhabited.

Laura Tempest Zakroff divides them into cognitive ghosts and repeaters. A cognitive ghost is aware of their surroundings and can communicate, interact with, and remember their past life. Repeaters are defined as residual energy, an echo from the past without awareness.[42]

Connecting with Your Ancestors

The usual perception of ancestors is family members who have passed away. However, this definition creates more questions than it answers. How far back in our origins can we go and still consider people ancestors? Are nonbiological family members also ancestors? And mentors?

In a more generalized way, ancestors are people who have passed away who are tied to your family's past in some manner, and they are bonded to you, generally to guard and guide you through life. From the perspective of the three souls and the three realms, the lower self of ancestors comes back to the Underworld to merge with the rest of them (see page 56). We can connect with those who have an energetic link with us.

Mallorie Vaudoise, the author of *Honoring Your Ancestors*, divides ancestors into categories.[59] A modified version of her categories includes:

The Dead, the Spirits, and the Gods

- **Blood Ancestors:** These are the ancestors linked to us through our DNA. This includes the ancestors we remember and those that we don't, going as far back as the first human in history. The ones who have been forgotten become part of the collective consciousness.

- **Lineage Ancestors:** We consider these ancestors family, but they aren't related to us by blood.

- **Affinity Ancestors:** These are people not related by blood who have had a significant impact on our lives, usually as mentors or inspiration.

- **Spirit Guides:** These ancestors, blood-related or not, are particular to a person and cannot be shared with others. Some stay with you throughout your life, while others accompany you during only a chapter of your life.

Ancestor work is entwined with cultural beliefs and personal perspectives on death and life. So, there are many perspectives on what constitutes an ancestor. Investigating and discovering what works for you is all part of ancestor work.

One of the most common ways to work with ancestors is to create an altar for them. This sacred space is consecrated to them and their memory; it includes a space to work with your ancestor and others, to remember and honor them (see page 138).

Researching your ancestors is one of the best ways to strengthen your relationship with them. Practitioners who work with their ancestors often create genealogical trees to help understand them. Their past lives will help you understand their signs and teachings better.

Some spirits have preferences about how they wish to be contacted and addressed. You can communicate with them via prayer, notes, burning messages, and simply talking at the altar. Offerings are also appreciated. These can be food or drinks, small presents, or flowers. If possible, personalize the offerings to something that matches their taste.

The answers to questions posed to your ancestors might come to you in different ways. Divination tools are a common way to channel them, as they allow the expression of a wide range of messages with precision. However, ancestors might also choose to send you messages in a different way, often related to their preferences and customs or their relationship with you.

ANCESTORS INCENSE BLEND

Incense is a common offering for the dead in many cultures. Its smoke attracts them, comforts our souls, and helps messages travel to their realm. I often use this blend as an offering before doing any ancestor work.

You Will Need
- ½ part myrrh
- ½ part frankincense
- 1 part dried apple
- ½ part sandalwood
- ¼ part dried cypress leaves

How to Make It

Put all the ingredients in a mortar and grind them with the pestle until they are well combined. Keep the incense in an airtight container to preserve it.

When you are ready to use it, place the blend over a lighted charcoal disc in a fire-proof container and burn it.

Use the incense and the smoke as an offering for your ancestors to make them feel welcomed and to show gratitude.

Good and Bad Ancestors and Ancestral Trauma

Ancestral trauma comes from the harmful events suffered by ancestors in their lifetimes. Wars, famine, depression, aggression, the loss of a loved one, and natural disasters are harmful events present in all timelines.[58, 59] These experiences can affect our relationships with our ancestors and create familiar behavioral patterns. They can materialize as bad advice, weak protection, or unconscious attitudes. The approach to solving ancestral trauma varies vastly depending on the issue. Some of the most common ways are journaling, shadow work, and healing rituals. You might also take action to avoid repeating the same situations in the future. And when possible, you might fix what caused your ancestors pain or the pain they caused.

Another problem often arises when the ancestors caused suffering to the witch who is interacting with the ancestor or to others. To heal this kind of event, it is essential to acknowledge it, actively work toward fixing the repercussions in the present (if there are still any), and work to avoid their repetition.

Remember that you are not forced to work with an ancestor who is damaging for you (e.g., abusive relationships). You can remove them from your practice. Sometimes, this can be nuanced, depending on personal circumstances and historical background. For example, a person who killed endangered animals that went extinct to feed their family without knowledge about ecosystem dynamics should not be judged by using the current knowledge.

Working with Different Spirits

The word *spirit* includes different types of entities from the Otherworld. It often identifies entities of the Midworld or lower or middle souls that are stuck in this realm. Devin Hunter, the author of *The Witch's Book of Spirits*, establishes three pillars when working with spirits: the art of mediumship, the art of flying, and the art of conjuration. Mediumship refers to gathering information from a spirit or channeling it, flying is the ability to astral travel, and conjuration is summoning a spirit.[32] It is important to identify the type of spirit you are working with, as not the same rules apply to all. Knowing the spirit you are working with will allow you to behave according to the circumstances and requirements of each situation.

There are many ways to communicate with spirits. My usual advice is that you attend séances with an experienced medium who can teach you before attempting it on your own. This can help you resolve any doubts beforehand and avoid possible future problems.

Before you attempt contact with the Otherworld, it is important to cleanse your space. Some practitioners also like to create a protective grid or circle, just in case they contact an unwanted spirit. If you are acting as a medium for a third person, make sure that they are comfortable and protected as well.[60] If you plan on channeling a spirit, don't allow them to take complete control of you.

The Dead, the Spirits, and the Gods

The CERT method is a common technique used to establish contact with spirits.[60] This acronym lists the basic steps for a mediumship session; however, its success depends on other factors. CERT stands for:

- Communication. Contact the spirit and establish a link with them.

- Evidence. The spirits prove they are who they say they are. This is usually done through a piece of information that only they could know.

- Reason. Establish why you are being contacted or why you are contacting them.

- Thank you. Appreciate their message, thank them, and close the session.

Animism and Allies

The etymology of the word animism is the Latin *animus*, meaning "soul, life." This strongly suggests its meaning: Everything has a soul. A division should be made here, as there are two beliefs: Everything *natural* has a soul, and everything, including human-made objects, has a soul.

Witches who follow this doctrine understand that plants, stones, spices, and bones are more than just ingredients; they are allies. Practitioners create a relationship with the object of their study, understanding it spiritually, and its energy becomes their companion and guide. While living and natural beings have an inherent spirit that grows and changes with them, the spirit of artificial elements is somehow different. They keep a piece of the soul of the being that created them, changing with their use.

Egregores

An egregore is a special type of spirit. Although egregores were initially linked to angels or watchers, modern traditions have started to use this word to define an entity or group mind that arises from humans united toward a particular goal.[61] As they originate from humans, they belong to the Midworld.

The more people who believe in egregores, the stronger they get; and they help the members who contribute to their formation. But egregores lose power when people oppose them, and they are weakened when people are not sympathetic to the cause. Sometimes they are classified as "artificial" entities or spirits, not because they aren't powerful, but because their power and overall existence depend on the actions of other beings.[62]

Faeries

Given their vast realm and popularity in folklore and witchcraft practices, faeries are familiar to us. And yet, the broad nature of faeries makes it tricky to classify them. Although they all belong to the Otherworld, they are often seen as inhabitants of the Midworld with strong links to the land (although not so deep as genii locorum). Some branches of the fae realm also venture into the Underworld.

In the fae classification, you can find many mythological creatures. This diversity marks faery work, as depending on the type (and sometimes on the individual), the fae have different laws, powers, and attitudes toward humans.

Faeries are powerful beings who appear in many different histories in almost all cultures, although their names and shapes vary. One of the central points that most stories share is the morality of faeries. Their rules are different from human rules, so some acts that we see as "bad" have good intentions on their part and vice versa. The fae realm is often described as a mirror of the human world, where reflected things are almost identical. Almost.

That doesn't mean that ill-intentioned faeries don't exist. In Celtic faery traditions, the fae are classified into *Seelie* (happy, blessed) and *Unseelie* (unhappy, unblessed). Although both of them can be dangerous or help humans, the Seelie faeries behave in a more benevolent way with humans, and Unseelie faeries are more malevolent.[62]

Safe Spirit Work

Spirits, like humans, have a variety of personalities and intentions, and they do not always have our best interests in mind. To avoid unpleasant situations, there are rules that you can follow to determine whether something is a "bad spirit" and how to proceed from there. What you feel when working with a spirit through your clair senses can be a good indication of their intentions.[3]

Before working with spirits, cleanse the space and establish protections. Some practitioners also cast a circle to delimit the workspace within that circle and make it easier to control. Some common indicators of a spirit with ill intentions are:

- The spirit shows impatience and aggressiveness. They resort to threats or "predict" something terrible happening to force you to behave the way they want.

- The spirit treats you as the chosen one. It tells you that there are many things only you can do or learn from them. They never give you any proof of this, and most of their information is not helpful.

- They try to isolate you from your friends or family or want you to give up on your life goals.

- They don't respect your free will and try to micromanage your life.[63]

If you encounter an unwanted spirit, there are several things you can do to get rid of them. First, ask them to leave confidently and firmly. Some spirits are oblivious to the fact that they are bothering you, while others will unwillingly agree to go. If they don't agree, cleansing the space might do the trick. It will disturb their energy and make them move. If they are still present, you can banish them. Banishing is often reserved for malicious spirits as a last resort.

CHOOSING A NAME

Names hold power. They are used to represent people or symbolize their energy in order to aim spells toward them. It is believed that someone who knows your complete name can access your energy. This becomes particularly relevant when you are working with spirits and even more relevant with faeries. Knowing your name gives them power over you. Because of this, some witches choose a different name for their magickal workings.

Another reason for a magickal name is separating your magickal workings from daily life. In the same way you cleanse yourself before a ritual, begin using your magick name once you enter a sacred space to symbolize your devotion to that activity.

The technique and the reason for choosing a magick name are entirely personal. Some choose one that shows devotion to a goddess; others decide based on what represents their personality. Others look for one that holds power, and others simply choose one that they like.

This is a modified version of a technique based on numerology that Ann-Marie Gallagher includes in her book *The Wicca Bible*.[5]

Write down your complete name, birth date, and time of birth. Use this table to assign a number value to each letter. Add up the numbers.

Add together the digits of the number you get. If that value has more than one digit, sum the digits. Repeat until you get a number with one digit. The magick name that you choose should match the same value.

For example, here is how this system works out for John Smith:

John Smith, April 2, 1973, 13:07 = 1 + 6 + 8 + 5 + 1 + 4 + 9 + 2 + 8 + 4 + 2 + 1 + 9 + 7 + 3 + 1 + 3 + 0 + 7 = 90 = 9

John Smith could use a name like Golden Raven = 7 + 6 + 3 + 4 + 5 + 9 + 1 + 4 + 5 + 5 = 54 = 9

Discovering and tweaking that name to make it fit can take a long time. Don't hurry; meditate and ask your guides. You will find the right one.

1	2	3	4	5	6	7	8	9
A	B	C	D	E	F	G	H	I
J	K	L	M	N	O	P	Q	R
S	T	U	V	W	X	Y	Z	

Worshipping the Gods

What are the gods? They are considered a type of entity that belongs to the Upperworld and has a connection with or is part of the Divine. We should note that some gods do not reside in the Upperworld (see page 77). However, this explanation does not entirely answer the question of their existence.

The truth is there is not a clear answer. Some people see the gods as archetypes of different energies; others conceive of them as the power gathered when many people worship something; others see them simply as higher-dimensional beings. Creating a relationship with the gods requires work and devotion, in the same way that having a strong, truthful, and meaningful relationship requires it. It is essential to keep in mind that the gods are not a monolith, and each one of them can require different behavior from us.

One of the best things about the craft's interpretation of deities is that it is a completely personal relationship. No one speaks for you; no one tells you how to act. This can also be scary because sometimes we can feel lost. The myths, traditions, and folklore give you guidelines about what to expect and what to do, but in the end, it depends on you.

This can feel overwhelming, particularly at first. *What if I do something wrong?* Keep in mind that the gods know about our imperfections and still contact us regularly. If you work with them in good faith, everything will be fine. (This doesn't mean they won't show you that you are in the wrong if needed.)

Usually, one of the key points of working with deities is studying their myths and their folklore. However, it is important to pay attention to the context. Gods were often used as characters in fables or other tales with a moral lesson. The society that told those myths often didn't have the same views on some actions that we do now. It is also not uncommon to find myths that have been misinterpreted, mistranslated, or modified through time.

Because of that, you also need to understand the society where those myths were born. Researching the gods and how they are (or were) worshipped will give you lots of information. Read and listen to invocations, poetry, and offerings; respectfully attend a ritual if possible; and remember that the best way to understand the gods is to experience them yourself.

But how do you choose a deity? There are two views on this question. The first is that you don't; they choose you, not the other way around. The second is that you don't need to feel a calling to work with them; if you are respectful, you can reach any deity that fulfills your needs in that moment of your life.

I don't think these answers are incompatible. Some gods will present themselves to you through signs and other manifestations, but that doesn't mean you can't look for advice from other deities when you encounter a situation that better matches their area of knowledge and action.

Lately, another way to see deities has reemerged. It stems from the notion that a "personal relationship" with deities arose in the context of Christian environments, while other pantheons did not create that type of relationship with their worshippers. Not all witches who work with deities worship them. Worshipping implies devotion, reverence, and adoration; working with them is seen as a partnership or collaboration. It doesn't mean that people who don't worship them don't acknowledge their divinity, but the relationship that they establish is more horizontal than vertical.[64]

Two of the most common and ancient ways of communicating with deities are offerings and prayers. Offerings are a way of showing devotion, deepening the relationship, asking for favors, paying pacts, or asking for forgiveness. Each deity usually has a set of preferred offerings. Prayers were present in many pre-Christian pagan beliefs. They are a way to use words or our mind, and sometimes rhythm and music, to communicate with deities. Sadly, many pre-Christian prayers have been modified, reconstructed, or completely lost, but that doesn't dismiss the effectiveness and power of this method.[65]

CHAPTER 8

RITES AND SACRED SPACES

From temples to sacred landscapes, places to practice spirituality have been searched for by humankind throughout history. We seek spaces to carry out rituals that connect us with our inner power and with the power of other entities. In Christopher Penczak's book *The Outer Temple of Witchcraft*, a sacred space is defined as a way to honor "the sacredness of the divinity, found in all things everywhere. We acknowledge that this space exists not only in the physical, but also in all worlds, and opens the doorway between the worlds, to be in conscious communion with the sacredness on all levels of reality."[45]

———

To Hestia belongs the world of the interior, the enclosed, the stable, the retreat of the human group within itself; to Hermes the outside world, opportunity, movement, interchange with others.

—Article "Hestia–Hermes: The Religious Expression of Space and Movement" by Jean-Pierre Vernant, excerpt from the book *First and Last: A Devotional for Hestia*[66, 67]

———

As you practice, you will realize that these definitions are flexible regarding the actual physical space considered sacred. Every place has the potential to be a sacred space for our workings. As witches, we use rituals and spells to help us modify the strings of fate, following techniques that channel and change energy; being in a sacred space helps us connect with energies and entities more easily. Many witches benefit from this by casting rituals in specific spaces, aligning the energy of their intention with the location.

In this book, we will discuss the characteristics of indoor and outdoor sacred spaces. It is important to note that not all indoor rites and tools are suitable for outdoors and vice versa. For example, it is not feasible to do a ritual that requires a bonfire indoors, and casting a circle with salt outdoors is toxic for plants and animals.

Sacred Indoor Spaces

Since humans adopted agriculture and became sedentary, they have built structures related to their spirituality. Having some degree of food security allowed them to explore their beliefs and create spaces focused on them.[9] It is not unusual to find temples built on other temples or sacred spaces. There are two main reasons for it: The first is it is easier to convince people to convert to a new religion and erase the old one if you don't alter their routine much. The second is because these buildings are constructed on sacred land or unique points of energy.

Having consecrated places that are centered on spirituality does not mean removing spirituality from your everyday life. However, some people seek a deeper meaning in areas where they can differentiate their spirituality from their routine. Temples fulfill this need.

Setting aside a part of your home for spirituality is a common way to integrate your beliefs into your daily life. House altars invite magick and deities into one of the most intimate parts of our life. These kinds of spaces are a way to commit to your path as well as a form of self-expression.

The Sacredness of Your House

It is not a coincidence that deities of the hearth, domesticity, and home appear in many cultures throughout history. Shelter is one of the basic human needs; it becomes an anchor point in our lives and allows us to grow mentally, physically, and spiritually. It becomes sacred.

Your home should be a place where you feel safe, and it should reflect your personality, like an extension of yourself. Your home is your temple. It should be treated with respect and appreciation. It is important to take care of it spiritually and physically; that includes care from energetic protection to maintenance tasks.

Arin Murphy-Hiscock names this type of magick hearthcraft.[33] For her, hearthcraft describes the home-based portion of spirituality: "Spirituality begins at home.

Honoring the hearth means honoring your origins, where you come from each day, and where you return each night." Hearthcraft focuses on the magick that hides in our everyday life. The mundane is magickal; our lives are magickal for the mere fact of existing. It is a nurturing and simple, yet powerful, view of the craft.

Working with this kind of magick means working with your home's physical space and embracing a nurturing path that focuses on personal development through the cultivation of basic needs and actions. Taking care of the sacredness of your home also encompasses its inhabitants, including yourself.

Working with Entities

When you incorporate your home into your practice, inviting deities and other entities to work with is common. They can be helpful, but it is essential to establish boundaries to create a peaceful cohabitation.

Josephine McCarthy suggests several valuable considerations to keep in mind when you incorporate your house into your practice.[13] I've modified and added to her list based on my own experience:

- **Cleansing and protection:** This is a step that everyone should take, but it becomes particularly important if your house is a part of your craft. You should cleanse it regularly to eliminate energies and presences that don't interest you. A protective shield will protect you and your workings from external forces.

- **Deities, spirits, and ancestors:** When you work with entities from "outside" the house, it is important to make them feel welcome so their power can flow through the place. Most practitioners do this by creating an altar where they can place their representations and offerings. In a sense, that would be their "room" in your home. Keep in mind that it might be necessary to establish boundaries for them.

- **House spirits:** These are a particular type of spirit linked to a house or a family (see page 133). Although it is important to establish that the house is yours and set boundaries, house spirits should be considered when you are making changes to the building structure or the composition of the household (e.g., the people, animals, plants, or spirits who live there).

- **Balancing the environment:** When you consider your home and all its inhabitants in your craft, it becomes a finely tuned environment that can be easily disturbed. To maintain balance, be mindful of your actions and how they impact the household.

Rites and Sacred Spaces

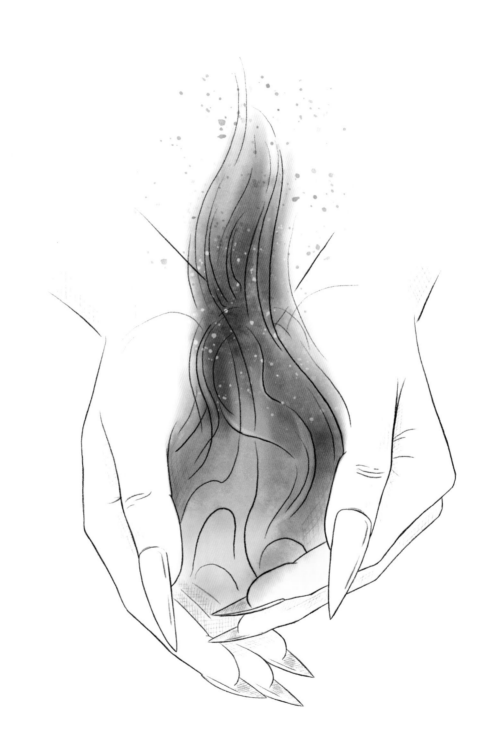

THE HEARTH FIRE

For many centuries, the hearth fire has been a focal point of domestic life. It keeps the home's inhabitants safe from the cold, away from the darkness, and fed with hot meals. The Greek goddess of domesticity, family, and the home, Hestia, was represented on the hearth of each house. She was always given the first offering for the gods, which highlighted her importance.

The hearth is also a way to symbolize that someone is at home and has not been forgotten. I like to keep a "hearth candle" on my altar with that symbolism. This candle is always lit (unless I'm asleep or out of the house), and it represents the eternal presence of the craft and the entities that accompany me in everything I do.

You can choose any candle that works best for you. It can be scented or anointed with oils that represent your desires for the house. I find it more practical to use a big candle in a glass container to avoid any potential mess or having to replace it too often. Before placing it on your altar, consecrate it and bless it:

> Might the fire of this candle
> Light the hearth of my home.
> His power protects and nurtures,
> Even if I'm here or I'm gone.
> So mote it be.

House Spirits

A house spirit is a type of entity linked to a home. House spirits are inhabitants of the Otherworld residing in the Midworld. They are often classified as a genius loci, minor deity, fairy, or goblin. I believe they possess enough distinguishing traits to be recognized as a distinct type of spirit.

The power or "life" of a genii locorum (see page 107) depends on a location. House spirits are entities in and of themselves and don't originate from human life (see page 56). But ghosts are associated with structures in different ways: They are anchored to the place, but their energy comes from their past lives as humans. Something from their previous lives connected a portion of their energy to that location.

I divide house spirits into two categories: those related to the house itself and those linked to the family who lives there. The first set will remain in the place regardless of who lives there, and the second will relocate with the family when the time comes. When talking to house spirits, I prefer to say they are linked to homes instead of houses because they are rarely found in houses that are not inhabited. They often have a playful attitude and can play some sick jokes, but in general, they tend to protect the people who inhabit the house so long as the people are respectful.[55]

That doesn't mean you can't find evil house spirits, particularly when they become angered after something happens to the family or the house. Because of this, it is vital to keep them in mind when making changes in the house or incorporating new members into the family.

Temples

A temple is a building wholly designated for spiritual practices. Temples' uses and aspects are as wide as the variety of human religions. However, all share some qualities. They are consecrated to an objective or a deity, and it is believed that a special force or entity is present in them, thus making its worship or petitions more relevant. Because of that, there are some actions reserved for temples.

Temples often act as teaching places too. Through their decoration or through the intervention of priests, priestesses, or other worshippers or devotees, people can come to understand better why temples are sacred to the religion and the main pillars of its beliefs.

It is not unusual for several temples to be built one on top of the other in the same place over time, as several spiritualties might see the location as an important and powerful point. In other cases, a faith may simply be reusing a building from a belief system that has become obsolete. Finally, building over older temples was a tactic used to remove a faith and establish a new one; by erasing the old temples and glorifying new deities, the space could be used to encourage (or force) the conversion of more people to the new religion.

Sacred Outdoor Spaces

Many pagan practices are held outdoors. For example, Celtic pagans created nemeta (singular *nemeton*) from the Iberian Peninsula to central Europe and Scotland. Nemeta were sacred places, particularly forests, where a wide variety of rituals were performed.

The power of the land is a strong aspect in many pagan beliefs. Some people argue that all natural places are sacred, while others think some are particularly relevant. From my perspective, nature is sacred as a whole and should be treated as such. However, there are points of high energy that can be differentiated from the rest. Working outdoors is a way to invite other forces and entities into your magickal workings. I find that it is often easier to connect with the element Water when casting a spell near a spring than when calling from a home altar.

This method of working with the environment is a way to connect with the powers of the land and reconnect with them. Josephine McCarthy warns in the book *Magic of the North Gate* that, as this person–land connection has been broken, it is easy for neo-pagans to fall into re-creating dogmatic patterns of early religions that are no longer applicable to our land or culture, evolving into "dressing up and role-playing with an added side of psychology." Her words might sound harsh, but I don't think they should be seen as discouraging or an invalidation of beliefs. They should serve as encouragement to find the true, raw form of your spirituality.[13]

There is absolutely nothing wrong with researching and adapting old rituals. However, we also need to rediscover our relationship with the land and forge a personal relationship with it and the entities that inhabit it.

There are many ways to work in outdoor spaces, and the best one for you will depend mainly on your goal. Possible goals can be divided into:

- **Rituals and spells:** You can consecrate a space for your magickal workings and collaborate with the advantages of the place to boost your rituals and spells.

- **Connecting with the land:** Working outdoors is a great way to become familiar with your surroundings. Learning the species that inhabit the place, their relationships, the climate, and the like will help you identify the place's energy and its changes.

- **Connecting with local entities:** As you get to know the land, you can begin to build relationships with the entities that inhabit it.

Most practitioners who practice outdoors seek hot spots or power spots in natural places of high energy. Some of these hot spots were used in the past and have remnants of previous use (e.g., stones from old buildings, shards of pottery, or bones), while others are considered "virgin."[13] Identifying a hot spot is not always easy. Legends and local folklore can give you a good insight into where hot spots are located, but you will need to rely on your connection with the land and your energy detection to identify them.

Creating and Using an Altar

An altar is a place that serves as the center of your magickal workings. Anjou Kiernan described altars in her book *The Book of Altars and Sacred Spaces* as "the heart of the mindful practice within a sacred space."[68] Keep in mind that altars are sacred workspaces; they aren't mere decorations. They gather the energy of their space, and they are windows to connect with entities and energies and should be treated as such.

You can have more than one altar for different workings. And there isn't just one type of altar; they differ depending on their purpose, traditional background, placement, and so on. You should decide on your intention for a space before working on it: Reflect on it, and write it down. Design your altar, and rethink it until you feel comfortable with the idea you have created.

After you have decided on the purpose of your altar, there are two main things to decide: placement or foundation and the items it will contain. Altars can be placed inside or outside your home, depending on things such as weather, privacy, and size. The foundation is where exactly you will set your altar (e.g., a shelf, a rock, or a table). Try to find a convenient place where you won't be disturbed during your magickal workings, which will help you feel safe and connected with the surrounding energy.

There aren't any items on a witch's altar that don't have a meaning, including decorations.

CONSECRATE AN ALTAR AND ITS TOOLS

Cleaning, blessing, and consecrating your altar and tools are ways to prepare for and devote yourself to magickal practice. Consecrating separates the space and objects from their mundane uses and connects them with your energy and the energy of the Divine.

Some witches prefer not to consecrate their tools or working spaces. However, I feel it is an important spell that transforms "normal" items into something sacred, and they should be treated as such. In this ritual, we will consecrate an altar and its tools.

You Will Need
- A bell
- Incense
- Blessed water, such as water that you have gathered from a natural source and consecrated on your altar by using your energy or tapping into the entities that work with you

How to Do It

Clean and organize your altar. Arrange the items you want to consecrate in front of you. Place the figurines or symbols of the spirits that work with you on the altar. Cleanse your altar and tools, as well as the surrounding space, with the incense.

Chime the bell four times, one per element, and ring it additional times for each entity you want present. Say:

Powers of the Midworld
And spirits of my craft
With your blessing and energy,
I consecrate these tools and altar.

Concentrate on your inner energy and tap into theirs too. Use it to draw a pentacle with your projective hand over the altar and the tools. Finally, sprinkle some water over them.

Once you are finished, chime the bell four times, once for each element, and ring it additional times for each entity present. Say their names and ask them to lend you their energy.

Decorations can have sentimental value or a symbolic meaning (e.g., colors or elemental representations) or simply make the place more aesthetically pleasant, making it easier for you to work on it.

Some practitioners decorate their altars to match the seasons, bringing a bit of the outside inside. This is particularly important for practices that work with natural cycles (see chapter 4). Altars are not a must for all traditions. However, as Christopher Penczak writes in *The Outer Temple of Witchcraft*, by creating an altar, you create space for the practitioner facet of your life and invite that energy into your daily life.[45]

Uses for an Altar

Although an altar is always related to your spiritual and magickal practices, there are many particular uses it can have, and each has different needs.[68] Determining your main intention will help you design and consecrate your altar.

Individual or Collective Use

Sacred spaces tend to change a lot depending on how many people are intended to use them, starting with the area they occupy. They are also often guarded with energy wards, a type of energy shield created by the energy present in the altar's place or by the people who work there. These shields can filter and interfere with the energy of the people who are working there, so establish energy wards with care. Another thing to keep in mind is whether the space is intended to be public or private.

Divine Devotion

It is important for many worshippers of the gods to have a place dedicated specifically for worship. These altars focus on offerings, acts of devotion, petitions, and communications with the deities. They often include images or representations of the god and candles that represent their presence. The design of the altar can vary widely depending on the deity.

Working with Entities

Although they are similar to altars focused on devotion to the divine, altars consecrated to entities are usually placed in locations that have a strong link to them or where their energy can be felt strongly (see page 107). Entities usually enjoy offerings and acts of devotion. Altars are the perfect place for this, and they help you tap in and channel the entities' energy.

Ancestral Veneration

This is one of the most emotional types of altars. These altars serve as a door to connect with the wisdom of your ancestors, and they are also a place to think about the loved ones who have left us and recall memories. In addition to offerings, candles, and tools, they are often full of photos, portraits, and other objects of sentimental value.

Rituals and Magickal Workings

Altars serve as a focal point for rituals and spells. They can be used to physically prepare the materials used in a spell (e.g., jars, herbs, or crystals) or work on its magickal aspect by raising energy and calling the entities you want to work with. These altars are often used as storage places for the tools, ingredients, and other materials you need for the magickal workings.

Liminal Exploration

It is easier to enter certain states of the mind, such as deep meditation or trance, if you dedicate a particular place for practicing them. The association gets written in our brains and makes it easier to travel the same path each time. Location is essential for these altars. You will need a quiet place where you won't be disturbed. It is also important to establish the necessary protections because you will be opening a door into the other world.

These altars are also used for divination rituals, keeping your tools in one place and allowing you to channel energies or observe the timeline safely. This makes sense when we consider that some divination techniques require some form of trance state.

Perfect Love and Perfect Trust

The phrase "perfect love and perfect trust" can be traced to *The Gardnerian Book of Shadows* and reappears in Aleister Crowley's work. However, its origins aren't specified. It is an important part of traditional British Wicca, but it can also be found in other craft branches.

"Perfect love" describes one of the highest spiritual achievements, a love that is unconditional, the love from the Divine.

"Perfect trust" is a consequence of perfect love. It implies that you are safe in the sacred space and that the people (or beings) in it with you are safe too.[70]

When entering a sacred space, these words are used as a key or password. In Wiccan covens, the reply is "All who speak such words are welcome here."[69] This saying implies entering sacred space with respect and good intentions, promoting the sacredness of that place.

Perfect love and perfect trust have evolved into a guideline for some practitioners in their craft. Some see it as a vow of commitment with their craft, deities, and other beings.

Rites and Sacred Spaces

Ritual Tools

Tools have power that goes beyond their symbolism or functional capabilities. The energetic nature of their materials and the energy that we imbue in them help us work with our magick.[45] As altars are one of the main workspaces for witches, most tools are stored there. Some have assigned places there to match their uses and correspondences, while others are kept there so they are conveniently in reach. Some witches also prefer to store functional items, such as matches, at their altar, while others keep them separate.

Your tools need to work as an extension of you, so you need to get familiar with their properties. A good piece of advice is to bond with a tool: spend time exploring and connecting with it. Remember that no tool is a must and that it is entirely possible to work without tools. They are an extension of your power that allow you to be more precise, to channel and multiply your energy.

Some of the most common tools that you can find at a magickal workspace are:

Altar cloth. A piece of fabric or natural fiber is used to protect the surface of your altar. Its color and designs can match your intention, match the season, or have another practical use.

Animal remains. This includes any of the elements left after an animal dies (e.g., bones, shells, or fur), as well as those that don't require the animal's death (e.g., feathers, shed skin, or antlers). They are used to tap into the qualities of that species.

Athame. This ritual knife is used for channeling and cutting energy. Traditionally, it is a straight, double-edged blade with a black handle.

Bell. Ringing bells is a common way to raise energy and help consecrate or reinforce a spell. Bells can be used to represent the element Air.

Besom. A besom is a broom made of wood and twigs and used for cleansing and "sweeping" the energy away. It can be regular-sized to cleanse bigger spaces or miniature for the altar surface.

Boline. This ritual knife is used to cut and carve or harvest herbs. Traditionally, it is a crescent moon–shaped, one-edged blade with a white handle.

Candles. Candles are versatile. They can be dressed with oils and herbs or carved with symbols. Their colors and scents are often used as a part of the symbolism of a ritual. They are used to represent the element Fire.

Cauldron. A container is used for mixing, holding ingredients, burning, and brewing. Depending on its intended use, it may need to be fireproof. Like besoms, you can find cauldrons in many sizes. It is better to keep separate cauldrons for brewing and burning.

Chalice or bowl. These are used to incorporate liquids into our magickal workings. Chalices are also used for drinking, and a bowl can contain other types of offerings.

Clothing. Ritual clothes are popular in many practices, and some covens require them. They serve as a way to separate the "ordinary" life from your magickal workings. As with altar cloths, their color and decorations can match the intention of the ritual.

Crystals. Crystal is an umbrella term for gems and stones. Each crystal is linked to a particular type of energy, and the crystal is used to incorporate that energy into the ritual. Crystals can also be used to channel or project energy and create grids.

Herbs and resins. Herb is an umbrella term for herbs, spices, and other plants used in the craft. They are common ingredients in potions, cleansing smoke blends, anointing oils, sachets, jars, and many other spells. Each plant is linked to a particular type of energy, and it is used to incorporate that energy into the ritual.

Incense and incense burner. Incense smoke is used for cleansing, blessing, and consecrating. Incense can be found mainly in three forms: sticks, cones, and loose. Choose your burner depending on your preferred type.

Mortar and pestle. This is a helpful tool, especially if you like to work with herbs and resins. It allows you to grind and mix them to create different powders and blends.

Natural items. These includes crystals, herbs, and animal remains, as well as soil, stones, bark, and the like. Each has its own correspondences depending on its characteristics. Be mindful when gathering these elements (see page 105).

Salt. Known for its cleansing properties, salt absorbs negative energies. It can be sprinkled around your altar or used to create energy barriers and cast circles. Please don't use salt outdoors where it will damage local flora and fauna.

Statuettes and other representations. These serve as a way to invite entities, deities, and different types of energies and inhabitants of the Otherworld into our rituals to communicate with them, worship them, work with them, or leave them offerings.

Wand. This tool is used to channel, concentrate, project, and redirect energy. Traditionally wands are carved from wood, but they can also be made from metals, crystals, and other materials. They are often decorated with stones and symbols.

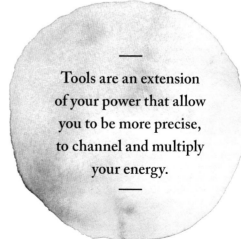

———
Tools are an extension
of your power that allow
you to be more precise,
to channel and multiply
your energy.
———

Symbols, Words, and Music

Powerful, ancient, and sometimes over-looked, these tools deserve a special section. The development of language drastically changed human societies and pushed their development forward. Words allow humans to describe our thoughts and feelings, reach agreements, share information, and create art.

In the craft, words are never void of meaning. They are tools that knit together rituals by specifying our intent and communicating with entities. In a sense, words are like a wand. Their power is derived from the will behind them. They are a tool that allows witches to sharpen their energy control. Because of this, it is important to choose words and language that allow you to express your will freely. Some rituals come with a predetermined set of words, but most don't. Choose the words and language that fit your needs best; they don't have to be "fancy" or "ancient."

When we work with magick and other realms, words become contracts. It is not wise to lie when trying to create a change in fate. In the best-case scenario, it will result in a misunderstanding with an unexpected outcome; in the worst, you will be upset.

Psalms, prayers, mantras, poetry, and other rhythmic forms for arranging words are particularly popular in the craft. As with many religions, this is often accompanied by music; repetition and tone help us reach the right mental state and energy.[65]

On the eightfold path (see page 47), music is considered a method for altering our state of consciousness. There are chants and melodies designed for that particular objective and others designed for special rituals, depending on your path.

Although I believe that lyrics impact the effects of music, I don't think that there is a one-fits-all type of "occult" song. Each person or group needs to identify the genre or artists that are suitable for their craft.

Both words and music are intangible things. To transcribe them into the real world, we use symbols. Symbols are written ways of representing concepts, but they also embody a particular type of energy in the craft. There are examples of symbols used for occultist practices that date back to the Neolithic era.[71]

There are many different types, and in this book I focus on runes, alchemical symbols, and sigils, as they are the most useful ones.

Runes

Legend says that the runes were revealed to the Norse god Odin during his quest for wisdom. Odin's obsession with knowledge drove him to several self-sacrifices, one of them being piercing himself with a spear and hanging himself from a sacred tree for nine days without water or food. After this offering, the runes deemed him worthy and revealed themselves and their magick.

The runes are letters that conform to the runic alphabet, a system used in central and northern Europe before the adoption of the Latin alphabet. There are three main runic alphabets: the Elder Futhark, the Anglo-Saxon Futhorc, and the Younger Futhark.

Rites and Sacred Spaces

The Elder Futhark is the most commonly used in occult practices.

The main difference between the runic alphabet and the Latin alphabet is that each rune represents a symbol and embodies energy. In Norse mythology, runes are described as having supernatural powers when used in the right spells. Divination using runes has also become popular in recent times.

The Elder Futhark has twenty-four runes. They are divided into three aettir, groups of eight runes dedicated to a deity: Freya, Heimdall, or Tyr. Each aett has different correspondences, and how we interpret their runes depends on those correspondences. Freya's aett relates to the role of the nurturer. Her runes are linked to the cycle of life, survival, and creation. Heimdall's aett is the warrior set, talking about the external forces that affect our lives and challenge us. Tyr's aett is the priest/king's aett, related to internal forces and transformation, getting in touch with knowledge and magick.

In addition to the individual uses of runes, you can combine them to create bind runes. Bind runes appear in ancient and modern texts made with various techniques, but all technique involve overlaying and unifying runes. You can create your own bind runes if you need the energy of two or more runes in a particular ritual.

Runes are more than symbols. They can even be considered an entity by themselves and should always be treated with respect. To access their power, like Odin, you need to dedicate yourself to them. Another note to keep in mind is that some runes have been appropriated and modified by far-right and Nazi groups. Context should be taken into consideration when working with them.

Alchemical Symbols
Alchemy is an old branch of science and philosophy. The history of alchemy goes back four millennia, and it was used until the eighteenth century. It is usually divided into three branches: Chinese, Indian, and Mediterranean, which includes Egyptian, Greco-Roman, Muslim, and medieval European practices.

Alchemy focused on understanding the world that surrounds us, developing the system of elements that act as building bricks of the Midworld, studying the planets, and exploring medicine and chemical reactions. Alchemists' scientific research was often profoundly intertwined with spiritual studies. Because of that, many esoteric and occult disciplines have adapted alchemy's symbols and findings. Some interpret them as purely spiritual, while others think they prove that spirituality, reality, and science can merge in a discipline.

The symbols used by alchemists weren't unified, and they often changed depending on the alchemist's education and even personal style, but some lasted and have become standardized over time.

ELDER FUTHARK RUNES

Aett	Name	Meaning	Correspondences	Symbol
Freya	Fehu	Cattle (mobile wealth)	Good luck, material wealth, abundance	ᚠ
	Uruz	Wild bull	Strength, courage, vigor, desires	ᚢ
	Thurisaz	Giant	Challenge, protection, danger	ᚦ
	Ansuz	God	Intelligence, communication, insight	ᚨ
	Raido	Journey	Evolution, progress, travel	ᚱ
	Kaunan	Ulcer or torch	Knowledge, healing, revelation	ᚲ
	Gebo	Gift	Generosity, partnership, help	ᚷ
	Wunjo	Joy	Joy, pleasure, success	ᚹ
Heimdall	Hagalaz	Hail (the precipitation)	Forces of nature, destruction, change	ᚺ
	Naudiz	Need	Necessities, resistance, delays	ᚾ
	Isaz	Ice	Isolation, stillness, blocks	ᛁ
	Jera	Harvest	Harvest, nature's cycles, growth	ᛃ
	Ihwaz	Yew	Strength, flexibility, divinity	ᛇ
	Perthro	Meaning unknown	Fortune, fate, mysteries	ᛈ
	Algiz	Elk	Protection, defense, instinct	ᛉ
	Sowilo	Sun	Success, energy, happiness	ᛊ
Tyr	Tiwaz	The god Tyr, victory	Leadership, victory, honor	ᛏ
	Berkanan	Birch	Fertility, new beginnings, creation	ᛒ
	Ehwaz	Horse	Travel, partnership, trust	ᛖ
	Mannaz	Man	Humankind, culture, mortality	ᛗ
	Laguz	Water, lake	Flow, intuition, mysteries	ᛚ
	Ingwaz	The god Ingwaz	Fertility, relationships, common sense	ᛝ
	Othala	Heritage, possession	Legacy, heritage, property	ᛟ
	Dagaz	Day	Awareness, clarity, truth	ᛞ

Elemental Symbols

These represent the four elements used in the Western branch of alchemy; other branches developed different elemental systems.

Air	△̶
Fire	△
Water	▽
Earth	▽̶

Planetary and Metal Symbols

The planets were associated with different metals, and the same symbols were used for both. Some changed over time, so it is possible to find them with different meanings depending on the context, but these are the most popular ones.

Mercury	Mercury	☿
Venus	Copper	♀
Mars	Iron	♂
Jupiter	Tin	♃
Saturn	Lead	♄
Sun	Gold	☉
Moon	Silver	☽

Processes and Zodiac Symbols

In the pursuit of creating the philosopher's stone, alchemists defined a process with twelve steps whose symbols were the zodiacs. This process of discovering the philosopher's stone was called the *Magnum opus*.

Aries	Calcination	♈
Taurus	Congelation	♉
Gemini	Fixation	♊
Cancer	Solution	♋
Leo	Digestion	♌
Virgo	Distillation	♍
Libra	Sublimation	♎
Scorpio	Separation	♏
Sagittarius	Ceration	♐
Capricorn	Fermentation/ putrefaction	♑
Aquarius	Multiplication	♒
Pisces	Projection	♓

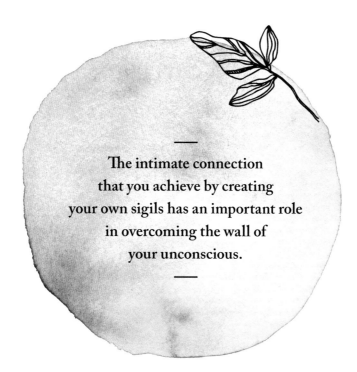

The intimate connection
that you achieve by creating
your own sigils has an important role
in overcoming the wall of
your unconscious.

Sigils

A sigil is a symbol created to embody a particular intention or goal. In the origins of sigil magick, they were used to represent and conjure spirits, angels, and demons. Over its history, however, symbol usage has evolved into a technique used to manifest all types of intention. Aidan Wachter defines the magick of the sigil as a method of coding information into a dense packet that can be gently slipped into our deep mind and avoid the "psychic censor," or the force inside us that opposes change.[15]

There are established sigils, mainly used when working with entities, but you can also design your own. In my experience, the intimate connection that you achieve by creating your own sigils has an important role in overcoming the wall of your unconscious. The book *Sigil Witchery* describes the benefits of hand-drawing sigils: Your brain is more engaged in the process of creating them, and it even activates the same "neurological paths" as it does when we are working toward an intention.[72]

Rites and Sacred Spaces

HOW TO CREATE A SIGIL

There are many ways to design a sigil, from using tables to combining letters or other symbols. They all begin with a clear intention, stated in positive terms. The intention should be concise and precise, with only one goal per sigil.

When you have drafted your intention, most design processes share common first steps: write your intention down and remove all the repeated letters and vowels. If the sentence is short, keep the vowels.

The next step will depend on the method you choose. In modern witchcraft, two techniques are popular in many branches and widely talked about: combining letters and using charts. To combine letters, simplify the letters into basic strokes, eliminate the repeated ones, and combine the remaining letters into a design.

When it comes to charts, there are many designs to choose from, such as the witch's sigil wheel (a modern version of the rose cross) or the Saturn square. You need to trace the words connecting the letters or the numbers that correspond with them for charts. If you use a witch's sigil wheel, you need to trace the words connecting the letters; there is one my book *The Complete Grimoire.*

If you use a Saturn square, find the numbers that correspond to each letter (table 7) to create a numeric sequence and then trace that sequence connecting the numbers in table 6.

4	9	2
3	5	7
8	1	6

Table 6. Saturn square

1	2	3	4	5	6	7	8	9
A	B	C	D	E	F	G	H	I
J	K	L	M	N	O	P	Q	R
S	T	U	V	W	X	Y	Z	

Table 7. Letter-number correspondences

Don't be afraid to play with shapes, calligraphy, and colors until you find the perfect sigil. Some people prefer working on several and deciding which one works for them during the activation process.[41]

Once you have decided on the sigil you will use, you need to charge it with your intention and activate it. There are different ways to do so, but one of the simplest is focusing on your goal or past experiences with similar energy and passing it to the sigil. Then burn it to free it from its physical form and allow it to work with the rest of the energy.

After the sigil is completed, you can write it and place it somewhere the energy will be particularly relevant. For example, a good place for a sigil to protect your home is at the front door.

Although you can stop working with a sigil, and likely you will forget it with time, it will still be imprinted in your subconscious. You cannot "uncast" it, so design your sigil with care. After a sigil's work has ended, thank and dismiss it and then forget it. Some people also like to burn it, the same way they did to activate it, or to trace it and release it in a water body (as fire and water are opposites).

Rites and Sacred Spaces

CHAPTER 9

BECOME YOUR OWN COMFORT ZONE

F inding a path that works for you should feel like coming home, a place where you are comfortable, understood, and safe. It should not feel forced, but something that comes to you naturally and is a source of empowerment.

——

What do you think of this sentence, Felipe? "Know yourself," Mafalda asks. "It's excellent! In fact, starting from today I'll begin putting it into practice! Yes! I won't stop until I know myself and how I am in reality!" Suddenly, Felipe gets sad. "Oh God! What if I don't like me?"

—Vignettes from Mafalda by Quino

——

This doesn't mean that your practice needs to be perfect: You will make mistakes. You will grow out of some part of your craft. You will doubt some aspects, and that's normal. Learning is a process, and there is always room for improvement. Keep exploring and doing what makes you happy.

This also implies discipline. When you want to get better at something, you need to put effort and time into learning and practicing. Experience will make you feel more comfortable with your craft as you become familiar with techniques and knowledge and explore what works and doesn't work for you.

Developing Your Craft

Magick resides inside you. It is inherent to you, and nobody can take it from you. That also means you are the only person who can tap into your magick and use it. In the journey presented in this book, you have learned to connect with all aspects of the trinity of mind, soul, and body; understand other realms; and connect with your surroundings and sacred spaces. Now is the time to put it all together, claim your power, and experiment with it yourself.

Your personal experiences with the craft will shape you and become part of who you are, in the same way that other events in your life leave an imprint and become part of you. Your experiences or your reactions to your experiences might differ from those of other people, and that's fine. Only you can walk your path. The author Devin Hunter defines it as a solitary process: "No one is ever going to understand precisely what it is that you find on your search for light; those are your mysteries. No one can trade places with you and do the work of studying and exploring them."[73]

Personal Gnosis

We denominate as personal gnosis the knowledge we acquire through our craft and interactions with other beings. Your personal gnosis doesn't depend entirely on you; it is often influenced by previous knowledge or beliefs that shape how we interpret reality.

As with any other knowledge, your personal gnosis should change when you encounter new proof or information. However, it will always be unique because no one else can experience the craft in the same exact way as you do.

Personal gnosis is often divided into verified and unverified personal gnosis. The first is a type of knowledge accepted by a leader that has become the "official" version. On the other hand, unverified personal gnosis (UPG) is personal experience that doesn't match the verified version. UPG has become increasingly relevant in many pagan and occult circles because it allows practitioners to explore and experience their spirituality firsthand, like a blank canvas, without previous conditioning.

Even if you follow an established tradition, you will encounter situations and challenges that only you can overcome. Because of this, it is important to lay out a solid base for your craft.

KAIZEN
Kaizen is a Japanese method of creating a systematic approach to gradually improving. The main idea is that small, doable, ongoing improvements create better results than big actions. Although it was created for business, this philosophy can be applied to personal life.

Become Your Own Comfort Zone

There are some questions that you need to answer to establish the pillars of your craft. It is often useful to write them down in a journal, book of shadows, or grimoire. I explain these aspects more in depth in my previous books *The Complete Grimoire* and *The Path of the Witch*.

- What attracted you to practicing witchcraft? What's your main goal?

- Do you feel a particular connection with a branch of the occult, a religion, or a type of witchcraft?

- Which set of ethics and rules are you going to follow? Are there rituals, materials, or tools you won't use?

- What are your views on death, reincarnation, and the afterlife?

- What are your views on the Otherworld and its inhabitants?

- Are you going to incorporate other entities into your craft (gods, the dead, spirits, faeries, etc.)?

- How do you connect with your ancestors; your background; and the local land, folklore, and culture?

- How would you define your relationship with the universe and Mother Nature?

Some of these points are better to clarify from the beginning. You can review them later if you feel the initial answers no longer fit your needs or your path. Exploring other branches, traveling, and getting in contact with people with different beliefs are all good ways to test if your answers are still fulfilling and still feel right to you.

Daily Practice

Daily practice has been a subject of debate in the recent years. Some witches think that it is a must and others don't. I believe that the craft should be an integral part of your life and it should be present every day, but that doesn't mean you need to go the extra mile for it every day. The same way I remove my shoes when I arrive home, I light a candle on my altar.

Daily practice also helps you to improve as it allows you to practice and exercise your magick muscles. It should not be an obligation but something that fulfills you. Sometimes it may be easy to prioritize your craft every day, but if something impedes you from practicing daily, it won't make your craft weaker than the craft of a person who can practice each day. Find what works for you in your life at this time.

Trial and Error

I'm a big advocate of getting informed and learning theory. I think there is a lot of wisdom that can be acquired from witchcraft authors, occult texts, and other reliable sources. However, at some point, you need to try it. Witchcraft is meant to be done. Experiment and keep track of the results.

It is possible that some things won't work for you. That's part of the learning process. Review the steps and see if something needs to be fixed when you try again or if that technique simply does not fit your craft.

Connecting with Others

Many withes find it helpful to share their experiences with other practitioners or even trusted people who don't work with magick. It is a good way to compare UPG, share resources, or simply debate the craft. From my point of view, it is enriching and does not go against the "keep silent" rule (see page 32).

The rise of the Internet has made it easier to find companions for your journey. Many forums, websites, and social media pages can help you meet people with similar interests. As with anyone you meet online, it is important to make sure that the people you encounter are trustworthy and that their beliefs are compatible with yours. Other ways to connect with others are attending workshops, taking courses, and visiting stores related to occultism, witchcraft, or even philosophy.

Finally, some covens have open celebrations and meetings that you can attend.

Motivation and Fear

The path of a witch is not easy. Many people feel attracted to it because of the media image of it. It is supposed to "put your life on easy mode," but it doesn't. Of course, it helps you to navigate some situations with more ease or get more insight, like other skills do. But it takes work, and life's difficulties don't just disappear.

Your motivation needs to be strong to advance your practice, but that doesn't mean that your reasons for practicing go unchanged. As we grow older, our goals and priorities change. Over time, your witchcraft, your spirituality, and your life will intertwine and become one: They need to be in harmony, or conflict will arise. See change as an opportunity to grow, and as you move forward in your journey, seek to maintain balance between your beliefs and your actions.

A witch is always learning, and with new information, you can encounter changes in your way of thinking or doing things. Your approach to these changes needs to be critical and flexible. If the evidence points in a different direction, there is no shame in changing the direction of your path. In the Thelema philosophy and religion, the concept of *true will* has particular relevance. It explains each person's role in the universe and the objective in their life. The universe will carry you through life if you follow your true will.

Motivation often comes in waves, and discipline and determination are what will really make you move forward. When the initial burst wears off, you need to remind yourself why you want to stay on this path: Define goals that encourage you. Find mentors who inspire you. Ignite the sparkle within you.

Keep in mind that doubts are also okay. Doubt about new and old information is a way to reassure yourself that you are on the right path. Just be careful; an excess of doubt might take you into a self-doubt spiral. Be critical but realistic, and keep a positive mindset. The path of witchcraft also comes with sacrifices. To create change, you need to exchange that energy for other things. Witchcraft author Sarah Faith Gottesdiener describes it as sacrificing the habits that don't allow you to focus on your craft and surrendering yourself to the change you are making.[36]

Pain will also be present at some point on the path. Pain is part of the human experience; everybody experiences it sometimes. Emotional, mental, and physical pains can be equally exhausting and distressing. Sometimes pain makes it impossible for us to carry on with our lives and concentrate on what is important. Pain is how our body communicates that something is wrong and needs fixing. But pain is an unpleasant sensation, and because of that, we try to avoid it.

Our brain has a sensation programmed to help us avoid pain: fear. Fear is our response when we perceive risk or a threat. Fear is unavoidable, and I don't think it should be avoided. It gives us important information about the situation we are facing. Maybe we don't have all the information about it that we need; perhaps our subconscious perceives something that we can't see, or maybe it is simply something unknown to us.

It is important to learn to differentiate between fear and intuition, as both are sensations that hit how we behave and can be confusing. One of the best ways to learn to differentiate is paying attention to your body's reactions. Fear triggers a different sensation than intuition, and it always points toward the harm potential; it indicates what to avoid. Intuition is often quick and tells us the direction we should follow; it doesn't create the same strong negative bodily response that fear does.

Dissecting a Spell

As seen throughout this book, magick can be presented and practiced in many ways. There is no single and correct way to live the craft. So laying out a definition of *spell* or *ritual* that fits all paths can be tricky.

In general, a spell is a process that allows you to tap into your energy, tap into the energy of other beings, or access other realms to create a change in the web of fate. Casting a spell combines and coordinates the concepts that we have covered in previous chapters. Keep in mind that all spells require a certain amount of mundane work for them to perform as you want. Magick usually takes the path of least resistance, so make it easy for it to achieve the goal you had in mind.

Christopher Penczak establishes "three keys" to spell casting: will, intention, and a method for directing energy.[45] Later he described them as altering consciousness, clear intention, and working with energy.[74]

Your will is not simply your desire; it is your connection with the Divine, the land, and your state of consciousness. I prefer to describe your will as your power to connect with the energy you need, whether from different entities or other sources such as nature or yourself. (This is in keeping with Penczak's second division, altering consciousness.) Your intention is how this goal will materialize, and you need to choose the appropriate method to cast the spell accordingly. Intention has a deeper meaning than want; it focuses on your will.[74]

It is vital that your intention is well defined before casting a spell. If not, the outcome might not be what you expect. In my book *The Complete Grimoire*, I suggest these questions to outline your true intention:

Is my intention well defined? Answering this question is not as easy as it might seem. Sometimes we need to question the real reason behind our desires. It is also important to ask yourself whether your objective is viable and to phrase it in a concise, positive way.

Do I understand the potential consequences of this intention and spell? Creating a change in fate can have many implications and ramifications that we didn't expect. I'm not (only) talking about it backfiring; it embraces the possibilities that can occur when things get in motion.

Does my intention contradict my morals? Your spells are part of your actions, and you are responsible for their consequences as much as you are for mundane decisions.

If the spell was designed by someone else, does it need to be modified to match your true intention? Premade rituals might not completely suit the precise details of your situation. You can tweak them so they are a perfect fit for you.

Am I ready to work toward my goal in the mundane world? You need to work on different areas of your life, including by taking actions in the physical realm, to aid your magick as it creates a change.[63]

Finally, when you design the spell, you must choose the best tools in your craft for it. There are many ways to design a spell for the same intention. It will depend on your tradition, knowledge, and practice. I define three main pillars for designing it: method, correspondences, and timing.

Methods
A wide range of techniques are used to combine energies and create change. Each method can be more or less appropriate depending on your craft and on the type of spell.

Amulets, Charms, and Talismans
Amulets, charms, and talismans are objects imbued with a particular energy that work when you carry them. They can also be placed strategically to intensify their effects, for example by putting a horseshoe on your door.

Become Your Own Comfort Zone

Some witches differentiate between the three words: Amulets are small items associated with particular energy because of their nature (such as a four-leaf clover); talismans are bigger items created with an objective in mind, usually shaped with relevant symbols, colors, and materials; and charms are items that you have charged with the energy you want them to possess.

Affirmations

Affirmations are sentences that concisely express your goals in words. They should be repeated (out loud or written) frequently. Keep them short, positive, in the present tense, and personalized or adequate to you, your goals, and your actual situation. Although not all practitioners share this view, I think they also have to be realistic.

Affirmations work on two levels: They introduce the idea into your subconscious, making it easier to work for it and allowing your subconscious to help you in your efforts, and they send the message to the universe to reinforce your intention.

Baths

Baths use Water as a carrier element that helps mix all the energies of the ritual bath in one place. As the energies "wrap" the person in the bathtub, they cover their skin, merging the energies of the items you include and covering the person with them. Some of the most common ingredients are herbs, crystals, oils, salts, moon water, and charms. Be careful when using oils; they can make the bath slippery!

Be sure the items you use are safe to submerge in water and aren't toxic. To avoid the mess of an herbal bath plugging your pipes, you can make a decoction first and add it to the bathwater, using bath sachets or drain filters.

Candle Spells

Candles are a powerful and versatile tool for spells. Candle magick is based on using them as vehicles to boost and send your energy to the web of fate. Candles are also used as offerings on altars as a way to invite and represent entities and spirits into our reality.

Candles are often used according to the correspondences of their color, scent, or shape. However, the energy of candle spells can also be defined by carving words or symbols on them or dressing them with oils, herbs, resins, and other substances. They can be used alone or in combination with other items.

Some witchcraft circles, especially Wiccan traditions, hold the belief that you should not blow out a candle and that, to complete the spell, the candle should burn down completely. In my experience, that's not appropriate for all situations. For example, my banishing spells work better when I blow out the flame.

Every time we work with candles, fire safety is a must. Never leave candles unattended, and be careful about the items you use with them. Some herbs can cause large flames, and some crystals might break.

Crystals and Grids

Crystals have become popular in many witchcraft practices, and their correspondences are well studied. You can use them by carrying them, placing them on your body, using them as materials in spells, and creating grids, among other techniques. A crystal grid is a way to arrange crystals, usually in a geometrical pattern, to connect and merge their energies. This can be more powerful than using crystals separately.

Stones and other minerals can also be incorporated into the craft as they also have their own energies. However, sometimes their correspondences are not as easy to classify and should be determined via experimentation. Folklore sometimes speaks about unique stones, such as hag stones or wishing stones.

Energy Projection

Energy projections consist of channeling your energy or energy from other sources into an item to charge it. This way, you can customize it to match your intention, and it is entirely personal. This technique can feel almost innate for some people, while for others, it takes a lot of practice (see page 11).

Glamours

Glamours are a particular type of spell that creates an illusion. They often rely upon other techniques, such as energy projection or charms, to be cast. The main difference with other magick methods is the change they create is only over the perception of others.

Infusion	Pouring boiling water over the herbs and steeping them for 5 to 10 minutes, depending on the herb. Infusions are commonly used for potions and spells intended for drinking.
Decoction	Boiling or simmering plants in water for 1 to 4 hours, usually in bigger concentrations than infusions.
Enfleurage	Extracting the oils of the plants by submerging them in oils or fats for 4 to 6 weeks. Sunlight can alter the process. Along with essential oils, enfluerages can be used to create salves and balms.
Maceration	Extracting the properties of the herbs by submerging them in alcohol for at least 3 days. Sunlight can alter the process. Maceration is also sometimes used for extractions using oil or water. An extraction using a mixture of water and alcohol is also called a tincture.
Distillation	This process uses heat to transform herbs' water and oil compounds into steam and separate them. The result is an essential oil. This process can be dangerous and should be done by a professional.
Incense	Incenses are herbal mixes made to be burned to release some of their properties into smoke. They are often a combination of herbs, resins, and a sticking ingredient to keep them together. However, you can also find loose incense (without sticking ingredients) or herbal blends (without resins).[75]

Become Your Own Comfort Zone

I like to describe glamours as the "makeup" of magick as their change is superficial and temporary. This doesn't mean they aren't useful or are less powerful. They are perfect for occasions in which you need to present a specific appearance. Still, you don't want it to be forever; for example, you might want to go unnoticed during an uncomfortable situation or look more beautiful on a date.

Herbalism

Herbs have many uses depending on their medicinal and magickal properties. In addition to using them in their natural state, many techniques have been developed to extract their essences and use them in the craft.

The right way to create herbal preparations will depend on the nature of the plant (if they are delicate, strong, have oil-based compounds, etc.) and the use you have intended for them.

I advise you to always take herbs seriously. There is a belief in some circles that "if it is natural, it cannot hurt you," but that's simply not true. Herbs can cause serious intoxication, medical interactions, or even death.

Knots

Knot magick consists of sealing your intention with every knot. It can be used to recreate knots with a particular meaning, such as Celtic knots, or incorporated into other crafts such knitting. Knots are also a way to create charms you can carry with you.

The type of cord that you use, which depends on the material, origin, color, and the like, can influence knot magick depending on its correspondences. Choosing a cord with a texture that makes it more difficult to untie is also important.

A popular craft is making witch's ladders, used as "meditation beads" or long-term spells. They consist of three braided cords and nine knots that secure different items related to the spell, such as feathers or stones, to the cords.

Sachets and Jars

This type of spell uses a container to concentrate the spell's energy. Sachets are created to permeate energy with the outside of the sachet, while jars focus on concentrating it inside and connecting with the goal in the universe. Either can be filled with a wide variety of items, including herbs, crystals, salt, photos, and other objects.

Sachets are often closed with a ribbon, and jars can be sealed with wax. Some sachets need to be fed new energy; when their effects start to wear off, charge them again with energy or replenish the ingredients.

MANAGING ENERGY

After you have explored the first steps of energy control in the exercise Receiving and Projecting Energy (see page 12), you can go a step further and explore how to manipulate that energy. The main focus of this exercise will be creating an energy ball with your own power, forming a circuit that crosses from your projecting hand to your receptive hand, passing through your arms and chest. (Note: This exercise is explained in greater depth in my book *The Complete Grimoire*.[63])

Once you have mastered the accumulation of energy, you will be able to project and shape it as desired. This practice is transposable to many other techniques that require raising, accumulating, and shaping energy, such as casting a circle to create a protective sphere around your working environment permeable to the powers and entities that work with us (but that rejects any unwanted external influences). The energy to cast the circle is obtained from inside yourself, but also from nature and the entities that work with you. Some practitioners consider it a modification of shielding (see page 176).

Create an Energy Ball

Place your hands in front of your chest, without touching them to each other, with your arms slightly bent, forming a circle as if you were holding a relatively big ball.

Create a circuit from your projecting hand to your receptive hand, passing through your arms and chest. Allow the energy to develop a stable flow, and then stop receiving energy and allow it to accumulate between your hands. At first, it will be chaotic and unorganized. Don't worry. You should feel the pull of energy from inside yourself.

Once you are satisfied with the amount of energy accumulated—aim for about the size of an orange—start gently moving your hands around it to shape it into a ball. Use visualization (see page 49) to help you in this process.

Once you have created a stable sphere, hold it in place with your hands under it and work on maintaining its shape without moving your hands.

When you finish your work, disperse the energy or return it to your body. Once you have mastered this process, you can incorporate modifications to make it more challenging, such as creating different shapes or pulling the energy from your surroundings instead of yourself.

Correspondences

Correspondences are defined as properties or uses that have been assigned to different materials, times, and energies, among other things. They are defined by culture and experimentation, and some might change depending on where you are located (see page 101). There are many books and websites focused on correspondences, but you will need to check if they are aligned with your practice.

Choosing the right ingredients, tools, and other elements during the process of casting a spell can boost or reduce its effectiveness. For example, to cast a candle spell to fall asleep easier, it's better to choose a blue candle than an orange one because blue promotes calmness and orange is the color for vitality.

The most common correspondences are for herbs, crystals, colors, materials, elements, weather, and planetary events. In each case, symbolism is intertwined with the interpretation of energy. They are complex concepts, and their use transcends the simple memorization of tables and keywords. In this section, we will cover them briefly. To pursue this area in depth, look for books that specialize on each topic to gain a deeper understanding of them.

Herbs and crystals are some of the most popular witchcraft tools. Their magickal correspondences are strongly linked to their properties in the mundane world. And their mundane effects can be as powerful as the magick they possess; research their toxicity and interactions when working with them.

Colors are how our brain interprets the reflection of different light wavelengths. A green object is green because it reflects the wavelength our brain associates with the concept "green" and absorbs the rest. Each wavelength has different energies, similar to brain waves. Culture also strongly influences color symbolism. For example, to represent "wealth," some people prefer the color green (associated with U.S. dollars), while others prefer yellow (associated with gold).

CORRESPONDENCES IN WESTERN WITCHCRAFT

Color	Correspondences
Purple	Spirituality, wisdom, magick, hidden knowledge
Blue	Calm, intuition, dreams, emotions, subconscious, healing
Green	Money, good luck, fertility, prosperity, rebirth
Yellow	Creativity, communication, positivity, wealth, imagination, learning
Orange	Happiness, opportunities, vitality, energy
Red	Courage, passion, love, danger, aggression, power
Pink	Friendship, children, love, nurturing, compassion
Brown	Stability, fertility, grounding, home, material decisions
White	Purity, truth, protection, initiation
Black	Protection, defense, cleansing, banishing

The correspondences of the materials used to create tools are also considered important, particularly those for wood and metals. For example, gold is related to solar/projective energy, while silver is related to lunar/receptive energy. Sometimes these correspondences are divided into two categories: herb/plants (and sometimes wood) or crystal/stone (and sometimes metal) correspondences.

The elements, as the building bricks of the Midworld, are a great way to connect with the raw energy of your intention. Each is a type of energy that has been studied extensively and has behavior that is well understood (see page 80).

Timing

Timing can be considered a part of correspondences or a part of methods, as it links particular energy to an event and should be considered in the designing process. However, I think it has enough importance to be its own topic. Coordinating your spells and rituals with events that share the same energy can help you boost their results. Some traditions consider timing a must, while others don't work with this aspect. I think it is important to review at least the most relevant events when planning a spell to ensure at the very least, they are not working against you.

The most influential circumstances for magickal workings are cyclical and can be predicted (see chapter 4). However, it is not unusual for several events with different energies to occur at the same time. If none of them is incompatible with your intention, prioritize them according to your tradition, abilities, and goal.

Timing is particularly relevant in paths that aim to connect with cosmic events or the rhythm of nature; I explain this in deeper detail in *The Path of the Witch*. Tracking these events and noting their energy and how they made you feel are great indicators that can help you decide on the importance of timing in your craft.

Apart from the events covered in chapter 4, there are ways to identify the perfect timing for your spell. In this section, you will find the correspondences for three methods that require less planning: weather, day of the week, and hour.

Weather changes are a reflection of changes in atmospheric conditions. Observing the weather, you can extrapolate these changes and their energy and incorporate them into your craft.

Not everyone agrees on using days of the week and hours as weeks and hours are anthropologic divisions of the time. However, many find them to be a useful way to connect with particular energies without having to plan weeks in advance for a ritual.

The correspondences of the days of the week stem from their correlation with deities. Each day is consecrated to one, and the areas they rule are considered the areas of influence of that day. Because of this, the correspondences will depend on your pantheon.

WEATHER CORRESPONDENCES

Weather	Correspondences
Sunny	Strength, happiness, vitality, positivity
Rainy	Growth, slow changes, cleansing, protection
Foggy	Introspection, glamour appearances
Cloudy	Reflection, calmness, self-improvement
Snowy	Divination, balance, transformation
Thunderstorm	Strength, courage, change, charging

CORRESPONDENCES FOR THE DAYS OF THE WEEK

Day	Planet	Greek/Roman Pantheon	Norse Pantheon
Sunday	Sun	Apollo/Sól	Sól
Monday	Moon	Selene/Luna	Máni
Tuesday	Mars	Ares/Mars	Tyr
Wednesday	Mercury	Hermes/Mercury	Odin
Thursday	Jupiter	Zeus/Jupiter	Thor
Friday	Venus	Aphrodite/Venus	Frigg or Freya
Saturday	Saturn	Cronus/Saturn	Saturday was considered the "bathing day"

Become Your Own Comfort Zone

For the division of hours, planetary hours have been regaining popularity. Planetary hours are part of a calculation system that assigns a planet and its correspondences to a particular time of the day that does not necessarily coincide with a "typical" hour.

To calculate the planetary hour, you need the exact time of sunrise and sunset. Then, divide the daytime or the nighttime, depending on when you want to cast the spell, into twelve equal segments. The length of these segments will change daily as the time for sunrise and sunset does.

Once you have calculated the length of these twelve hours, assign them a ruler planet, starting from the planet that rules that day of the week (check the previous table) and following this order: Sun, Venus, Mercury, Moon, Saturn, Jupiter, Mars. Cast your spell during the time ruled by the planet that best fits your intention.

Write It Down

Many traditions encourage keeping some kind of record of magickal information of your personal experiences with the craft. Two of the most common examples are books of shadows and grimoires. I think that records are the only tool that are an absolute must in the craft. Our brain is programmed to forget things that we don't review often; a record is written permanently. Plus, it allows you to find patterns that would have gone unnoticed otherwise. Even if you can keep all the information in your head, a record will free that mental space designated to "things I should not forget" and allow you to use it for different things.

There are different ways to approach a magickal record. Some covens have a shared grimoire that stipulates common rules and beliefs while each member keeps a separate notebook. Other traditions pass down a book from teacher to apprentices, and every generation contributes. Modern witches have incorporated other methods for keeping records, such as online documents.

What to incorporate in your records and how are up to you. I find it handy to keep separate records for different topics. It makes it easier to get organized and find what you are looking for quickly. You can find premade grimoires that can work well as starter guides, but they aren't as personal as those you make yourself.

These records are a tool for the craft and should be treated as such. Many people consider them sacred. It is important to be respectful of the meaning and the contents. They are often blessed, consecrated, and protected.

RECORD SHEET

Premade sheets that allow you to fill the blanks as you go without interrupting the ritual are a useful tool if you want to keep a record of your practice. Their layouts depends on your practice and what you want to register (e.g., a spell, a séance, or a divination session).

Some of the most common sections include: date, relevant astrological events, location, type of ritual, people who participated, entities present, materials used, sensations during the ritual, and relevant events.

I like to include a section to be filled in after the ritual generates an effect to be able to compare the outcome with the process.

You can design your sheet to match your needs. Try the example on the opposite page as a base for creating your own records.

Date: Time: Day of the week:

Location:

Sun sign: Moon phase: Moon sign:

Other astrological events:

Type of work:

Altar setup:

Tools and materials used:

Divination:

Offerings:

Deities/entities present:

Process of the spell:

Outcome:

Notes:

Ethics

As with many other things in life, what's right and wrong in the craft varies to some extent according to each practitioner. Some things might be apparent, but most of our actions fall into a gray area. Your ethics regarding magick should be aligned with your ethics for mundane actions; if not, they will clash, and your results won't be what you desired.

Establishing the bones of your ethics might seem easy, but questions will arise and they will make you consider your choices and decisions. It is entirely normal to tweak your ethical guidelines as you deepen your knowledge or your life changes. In fact, I think it is important to review where we stand when our beliefs are challenged.

Assuming the consequences, good or bad, intended or unintended, of our actions is a must in the craft. It is easy to feel disconnected from our magick when the outcome is not intended. Taking responsibility for your workings is a requirement for making progress in your craft.

Along your path, you will meet witches who align with your ethics and others who don't. It is up to you to decide whether those differences affect your relationship or not. My advice is to establish boundaries with other practitioners about topics you don't want to discuss or participate in.

Ethical Considerations for Your Craft

Each witch is different, but there are points about which almost all practitioners have to know where they stand. This list is modified from the book *Rebel Witch* by Kelly-Ann Maddox.[76]

Different Cultures and Traditions

Participating in a faith that you don't share is viewed differently depending on whether it is an open or closed ritual. It is important to attend both types of rituals respectfully and respect their boundaries. Open rituals are meant for any people to attend. Closed rituals are reserved for members of a faith or even just a select group of those members; it is likely that you need to be invited and sometimes initiated to attend.

There are also closed religions or practices. They come from cultures that have been oppressed throughout history, and their beliefs and customs have suffered attempts of being erased. When outsider groups incorporate and modify those beliefs, it can violate the boundaries of marginalized groups because their beliefs and sacred practices are being taken advantage of by the system that oppresses them.

Learning or obtaining items from such traditions should always be done from members of that culture, supporting their work and respecting their decision if they don't want to share. Another reason to be careful with this type of magick is that the lack of context can quickly spread misinformation and distort the original ritual, changing the outcome.

Free Will

Interfering with the free will of others includes a myriad of types of magick. The usual definition for interfering with free will is forcefully changing a person's actions, thoughts, or feelings. Some of the most usual problematic spells are:

- Love spells, in particular those that force a person to love somebody or stop loving them. The main concern is that those feelings are "fabricated" by the caster and not real. They also raise the question of why you would want to expose someone you appreciate to that. Plus, they backfire easily.

- Binding spells aimed at preventing a person from doing a specific action. The controversy here primarily arises when they are used to stop someone from hurting others or themselves.

- Spells for others without their permission. Even if they are well intended, these are seen as a step too far for some witches. Asking beforehand is usually the safest way to proceed. It also addresses the handicap of not knowing completely what's happening in somebody's life and messing with their final goal or simply backfiring and harming them.

Hexing and Cursing

This kind of magick focuses on harming a particular person. The reasons behind casting these spells vary widely: jealousy, hatred, justice, revenge, teaching a lesson, and so on. In general, they are a way to punish a person.

The usual argument against hexes and curses is that you are placed in the position of judge, jury, and executioner, and sometimes mistakes happen. Some witches are against any type of harm, believing that this gift should not be used to cause pain. However, this isn't an argument against self-defense or standing up for yourself. In those circumstances, you can focus more on finding a different way, such protective rituals, binding spells, or magick aimed to quicken the consequences of someone's wrong actions.

Another controversial point about hexes and curses is the negative energy they raise. Some witches say it will permanently become attached to or come back to the sender, making them "pay the price." Others believe having the right skills and using protective steps make hexing and cursing completely safe. If you choose to use this kind of magick, a caution holds true here: They are a type of spell that easily backfires because they are often cast in the wrong mental state.

Environmentalism

You have probably realized this is a topic I have strong opinions about. A big part of my life is focused on studying, protecting, and improving the environment.

Many witches work with nature's powers; it is a big part of our magick. Even the witches who don't work with natural magick are still part of nature. Taking care of Mother Earth has become more than a question of protecting our power and the life on this planet. It is a matter of survival.

It is also important to understand the main problem stems from global politics and companies, and there is only so much one person can do. We need a worldwide radical change. However, there are also small things you can incorporate into your craft to be proactive.

Helping Others

Due to the power that a witch has, some consider it a must to help people in need, even considering it against their beliefs to charge money for their services. Others see it as any other skill and that they are not obliged to do anything. Helping others can overlap with not harming, and some witches incorporate it into their daily life and their craft, for example, by buying from ethical sources.

—

We don't need a handful of
people doing zero waste perfectly.
We need millions of people
doing it imperfectly.

—ANNE-MARIE BONNEAU

—

Creating a Change in Fate with Magick

You have the tools and power you need to develop and elevate your magick. Now is the time to put it into practice. Here are some basic methods to keep in mind when working with energy and entities. Don't let the word basic make you dismiss these practices; it doesn't mean they are only for beginners. It means they work as an essential and necessary foundation for many magickal workings.

Banishing

Banishing is a technique used to dismiss or remove any unwanted energy, entity, or other being. This is a way to disrupt energy, and banishing can even be used to affect the web of fate and remove something that interferes with your goals. The ethics of this last use are often debated.

Cleansing

Cleansing can be considered a type of banishing because it removes energy, but it is only used as a way to energetically clean tools, spaces, or beings to avoid interferences of other types of energies in your practice. This type of spiritual hygiene should be done regularly to prevent possible problems.

There are many cleansing methods, such as water, salt, soil, fire, crystals, sound, and smoke. When choosing, keep in mind the possible physical damages your method can cause to what you want to cleanse. For example, some crystals are affected by water and heat, so it is better to use sound or smoke techniques with them. Salt and iron are commonly used to disrupt and remove energies. Because of that, they are a helpful tool when dealing with unwanted entities. Some people always keep them near when walking the axis mundi and working with OBE.[32]

I recommend cleansing before any ritual or spell if you feel a negative buildup and if it has been a long time since the last time you cleansed. Depending on the ritual you perform, you might also want to cleanse after, especially if you have encountered baneful magick or dangerous entities.

Charging

Charging is the process of imbuing an item with the type of energy that interests us for a particular goal and increases its bond with us. Some items, particularly crystals, can also be programmed, focusing their energy toward a specific intention. There are many ways to charge an item, depending on the purpose and the material it is made of. Some of the most common ones are your energy, natural light, the elements, crystal grids, or sigils and other symbols.

There is some debate regarding charging crystals, as some people think it can affect their "natural" vibrations and prejudice their energy flow. Instead, it is better to simply cleanse them and allow them to work as they are supposed to. On the other hand, for some practitioners, charging and programming crystals is a way to emphasize their energy and focus on their goal.

Protection

We can affect the world that surrounds us with magick and energy, and we also feel the effects of other beings and events on us. These actions are not always deliberate, but they still affect us. Being in other realms and interacting with people, entities, objects, or places with particular energy can affect us.

Protection magick is designed to protect us from attacks, deliberate or not. One of the best methods for this is called shielding. It consists of creating an energetic shield around yourself to repel unwanted interactions. Advanced shielding techniques create several layers with different purposes. Other common forms of protection are charms, talismans, and amulets—objects that, due to their correspondences or a spell that has been cast on them, have a protective effect over the wearer or the place where they are.

Grounding

Grounding is a process that allows us to be fully aware of the present and realign ourselves with our surroundings and our inner world. It is about regaining full consciousness to decide with full awareness. Grounding increases our focus and calm, which becomes important when working with magick. This method can be considered a form of meditation and part of the eightfold path (see page 47). However, I think it is an important first step to creating the state of consciousness your ritual requires.

Divination

Divination consists of seeking answers or knowledge about the unknown by using your intuition or tapping external forces. There are different ways to approach divination depending on the results you are looking for or your witchcraft tradition, ranging from seeking self-understanding to communicating with spirits to gaining information about past, present, or future events.

Many tools, such as tarot decks, pendulums, runes, and scrying, can help you channel these answers. One tool might be more suitable than another depending on your use of it and your skills. When using divination to look into a particular situation and its development, it is important to remember our actions can affect how events unfold. Divination is a useful tool, but it should not dictate all your actions.

Become Your Own Comfort Zone

LIGHT SHIELDING

Light shielding is one of the easiest and most common protection rituals as it focuses on visualization and energy projection. It can be done as part of your routine or cast for a particular occasion, such as traveling the axis mundi.

You can create a more intricate energy shield by layering. You can create protective layers with different intentions or linked to different entities. Specialized protections are often stronger than their generic versions, and they offer the advantage that, if one breaks, the rest are still there.

Cast Your Shield

Cleanse yourself before casting an energy shield to avoid unwanted energies getting stuck inside.

Visualize a shield of light that completely covers you. I usually conceive of it as a bubble around me. It is shiny, and it is permeable to what I want but strong as a rock against attacks.

Once you have it in your mind, project your energy to fill and create it. If you work with entities or other energy, you can call them to help you materialize your shield.

Some shields are meant to always stay in place. Others have a particular goal and once it is fulfilled, they can be taken down. To do this, visualize the shield and dispel the energy or reabsorb it, depending on the source you used to cast it.

If your light shield is meant to be maintained, check it often. Although shields are a great tool, continued attacks can damage them, and they will need to be recast.

FAQ and Troubleshooting

As you practice, challenges and doubts will arise. It is normal and inevitable; it happens during the learning curve of any practice. Experienced practitioners also encounter this. Although the notion of not being alone can bring some comfort, it does not solve the problem itself. In this section, you will find some of the most common "bumps in the road" you may encounter.

Losing Passion

Sometimes you might feel very involved with your craft, and other times you might feel disconnected. This is normal. Humans go through phases with their interests. Sometimes they match a period of time when we feel down or are more stressed for different reasons. Others just happen. I think the best way to tackle a loss of passion is by getting inspired: Read a book out of your usual practice. Look into other peoples' practices. Go to group rituals or celebrations. Review what made you want to start this path to begin with, and reignite the flame.

It is also important to try to identify why your passion is low. Is it a lack of time? Of motivation? Of discipline? Do this from a nonjudgmental point of view; talking down to yourself won't help.

If nothing seems to work, you might have to consider whether your path no longer works for you. It is okay to change and stop doing what no longer resonates with you and brings you happiness. And it is also fine if you feel the need to go back to those activities later. Life is a flowing change; resisting it won't do you any good.

Not Believing in Your Power or Magick in General

Is magick real? This is the question I get asked the most. Your power and ability to tap into other energies have a strong component of will and subconscious, so doubts will weaken them. I'm not saying you should not question the craft; to the contrary, critical thinking is a must for finding what works for you.

The best approach is being curious and open-minded but also questioning. This mindset allows you to explore and discover without the fear of being out of touch with reality. Your experiences are unique.

Judgment

The term *witch* has been used to oppress people for a long time, and today it still has a stigma attached to it. It is essential to educate people and reclaim the word. However, many people still see it in a bad light and can react badly to it. You don't need anybody's permission to practice, but your safety always comes first. Not being open about your craft is a decision that is as good as any other. If you are unsure about the reaction someone might have about your practice, try introducing it slowly with the most mainstream topics.

Imposter Syndrome and Imitation

Having access to large amounts of information and observing other peoples' paths has many benefits. At the same time, it can also trigger a feeling of "not being enough" or even imposter syndrome when you doubt your talents and think you are faking them. Keep in mind the content you see online is curated and does not represent reality.

It is also healthy to ask yourself how much social media influences your craft. It is not unusual for trends to appear where everyone seems to practice in the same direction, only then to change to a different direction sometime later. Don't be afraid to question the consensus. Research and think critically and carefully about information you see online.

Spells Not Working or Backfiring

The negative impacts of working with magick are things that worry most beginners. Although negative impact is a possibility, it is also a scare tactic used by people who don't understand or like magick. It is always important to be careful and mindful with your craft and responsible for the consequences of your magick workings.

Some of the most common causes for spell failures and backfires are:

- Badly specified intention. If your intention wasn't matured carefully, it might not represent your goal accurately or it might represent it negatively. It might also be an unrealistic goal that cannot be achieved through the means you chose.

- Lack of mundane work. Magick working needs its counterpart in the mundane reality. Your real-world actions will open the way for your magick to act.

- It manifested in an unexpected way. This one is often related to a poorly specified intention. Magick tends to take the path of least resistance, and that might be an outcome you weren't expecting or even one that goes against your wishes. Let's say you asked for more money; your boss could call on your birthday weekend you because your job is short-staffed.

- You need to be more patient. Witchcraft is not instantaneous. Maybe it is not that your spell didn't work, but that it needs more time to manifest its effects.

- Not enough practice or too much self-doubt. Ability, experience, and confidence raise the probability of your spell working exactly as expected. Don't give up, and keep practicing.

- Wrong technique. Maybe you simply made a mistake when casting a spell, and it wasn't done correctly. Review your ritual record sheets to find out where it went wrong.

It is always better to plan your spells well to avoid these situations. However, if you encounter yourself in the scenario when you need to uncast a spell, two of the most common ways to do so are:

- "Rewinding" the spell. This consists of casting the spell again but starting from the end and moving toward the beginning. If possible, use the materials involved in the first spell.

- Using the contrary tools. Cast the spell again, but using the opposite of every tool. For example, if you burned your petition, write the contrary and dissolve it in water.

Although this option might seem like a safety net, some things cannot be undone entirely, particularly if they have already manifested their effects.

Dangerous Members of the Community
Although this is not inherent to or unique to the witchcraft and occult community, it is not uncommon to find people who want to take advantage of others using their beliefs. Be aware of people who make odd demands about your body, actions, emotions, money, belongings, or anything else that is private to you. You should never feel coerced into participating in any ritual or activity.

Sometimes these people can be very persuasive, and you might not realize their motives in the beginning. Keep an eye open for techniques such as isolation, love-bombing, generating a division between the group and the world, controlling behaviors, and dependency. If you spot these behaviors, distance yourself from the person and ask for help from a trusted person or a group. You do not have to handle this alone.

The Path Is Made by Walking

I want to finish this book with some encouragement: The path is rewarding, nurturing, and comforting. Sometimes, it can also be challenging, confusing, and obscure. And that's okay, because it expands your frontiers like no other journey. Seeking the company and wisdom of others will keep it from being lonely.

Don't resist change; instead, adapt and flow. Train your curiosity and your critical thinking because the process of learning never ends, and that's exciting! There will be difficulties, but they are all worth it if the craft fulfills you and helps give more meaning to this adventure we call life.

And if one day you decide the craft no longer aligns with your necessities, it is okay. Be grateful for the time you shared. Magick will be waiting for you if you decide to come back.

SELF-DEDICATION RITUAL

A self-dedication ritual is a pact with yourself and the entities and energies that accompany you on your path. It is a rite present in many solitary traditions. In a way, it could be compared to initiation rituals in covens and other groups. It is a way to dedicate yourself firmly to your path.

You don't need to do a self-dedication ritual to start working with witchcraft. In fact, it is advisable to study and practice first, so you know it is the right decision and that you are ready for it. Some Wiccan traditions and other witchcraft branches advise spending a year and a day studying and familiarizing yourself with the practice before the self-dedication ritual.

You Will Need

- Salt
- Fresh rosemary
- Self-dedication vows
- Myrrh and frankincense incense
- Cauldron
- Charcoal disk
- Salt
- White candle
- Paper and pen
- Blessed water or anointing oil

How to Do It

Mix the salt and fresh rosemary. Use the mixture as a scrub in the bath or shower to cleanse yourself and eliminate unwanted energies.

Mix myrrh and frankincense in equal parts. Burn the mixture in a cauldron using a charcoal disk.

Use its smoke to cleanse your space. Sprinkle some salt through the space.

Invite any deities or entities you think should be present.

Light the white candle, and while the resin blend burns, start working on your vows and writing them down on paper. These are your commitments to your craft, your beliefs, and your deities. It can be difficult to put everything into words, so it will help you to have this written down.

Observe the candle and feel the warmth of its light. Say your vows out loud. You can sign them with your name or use your magick name (see page 123).

Anoint your forehead, chest, and belly with the blessed water or anointing oil. Light your paper with the candle's flame and place it inside the cauldron.

ENDNOTES

1. Crowley, Aleister. *Magick in Theory and Practice.* London: Dover Publications, 1929.

2. Yang, Jwing-Ming. *The Root of Chinese Qigong: Secrets for Health, Longevity & Enlightenment.* Boston: YMAA Publication Center, 1997.

3. Auryn, Mat. *Psychic Witch: A Metaphysical Guide to Meditation, Magick & Manifestation.* Woodbury, MN: Llewellyn, 2020.

4. Wong, Kiew Kit. *The Art of Chi Kung: Making the Most of Your Vital Energy.* Rockport, MA: Element Books, 1993.

5. Gallagher, Ann-Marie. *The Wicca Bible: The Definitive Guide to Magic and the Craft.* London: Godsfield Press, 2005.

6. Fries, Jan. *Seidways: Shaking, Swaying and Serpent Mysteries.* Wiltshire, England: Mandrake of Oxford, 1996.

7. Foote, Jennifer. "Trying to Take Back the Planet." *Newsweek*, February 5, 1990.

8. Jepson, Paul, and Cain Blythe. *Rewilding: The Radical New Science of Ecological Recovery.* London: Icon Books, 2020.

9. Duru, Güneş. "Sedentism and Solitude: Exploring the Impact of Private Space on Social Cohesion in the Neolithic." In *Religion, History, and Place in the Origin of Settled Life*, edited by Ian Hodder, 162–85. Louisville, CO: University Press of Colorado, 2018.

10. Kesebir, Selin, and Pelin Kesebir. "A Growing Disconnection from Nature Is Evident in Cultural Products." *Perspectives on Psychological Science* 12, no. 2 (2017): 258–69.

11. NASA, "Scientific Consensus: Earth's Climate Is Warming." Global Climate Change: Vital Signs of the Planet. Last Modified May 5, 2022. https://climate.nasa.gov/scientific-consensus/.

12. Brower, Vicki. "Mind-Body Research Moves Towards the Mainstream." *EMBO Reports* 7, no. 4 (March 2006): 358–61.

13. McCarthy, Josephine. *Magic of the North Gate: Powers of the Land, the Stones and the Ancients.* Exeter, UK: TaDehent Books, 2020.

14. Parma, Gede. *By Land, Sky & Sea: Three Realms of Shamanic Witchcraft.* Woodbury, MN: Llewellyn, 2010.

15. Wachter, Aidan. *Weaving Fate: Hypersigils, Changing the Past & Telling True Lies.* n.p.: Red Temple Press.

16. Breuning, Loretta Graziano. *Habits of a Happy Brain: Retrain Your Brain to Boost Your Serotonin, Dopamine, Oxytocin & Endorphin Levels.* Avon, MA: Adams Media, 2015.

17. Mattson, Mark P. "Superior Pattern Processing Is the Essence of the Evolved Human Brain." *Frontiers in Neuroscience* 8 (August 22, 2014).

18. David, A. P. "Homer and the Soul." Classical Wisdom, November 16, 2012. https://classicalwisdom.com/people/poets/homer-soul/.

19. Zakroff, Laura Tempest. *The Witch's Cauldron: The Craft, Lore & Magick of Ritual Vessels.* Woodbury, MN: Llewellyn, 2017.

20. Punset, Elsa. *El Libro de las pequeñas revoluciones: 250 rutinas exprés para mejorar tu día a día.* Barcelona: Ediciones Destino, 2016.

21. Pradas, Lidia. *The Path of the Witch: Rituals & Practices for Discovering Which Witch You Are.* Beverly, MA: Fair Winds Press, 2021.

22. Lévi, Éliphas. *Transcendental Magic: Its Doctrine and Ritual.* England: Rider & Company, 1896.

23. Orapello, Christopher, and Tara-Love Maguire. *Besom, Stang & Sword: A Guide to Traditional Witchcraft, the Six-Fold Path & the Hidden Landscape.* Newburyport, MA: Weiser Books, 2018.

24. Penczak, Christopher. *The Inner Temple of Witchcraft: Magick, Meditation, and Psychic Development.* Woodbury, MN: Llewellyn, 2002.

25. Taylor, Astrea. *Intuitive Witchcraft: How to Use Intuition to Elevate Your Craft.* Woodbury, MN: Llewellyn, 2020.

26. Dominguez, Ivo, Jr. *Keys to Perception: A Practical Guide to Psychic Development.* Newburyport, MA: Weiser Books, 2017.

27. Stone, Anna. "Rational Thinking and Belief in Psychic Abilities: It Depends on Level of Involvement." *Psychological Reports* 118, no. 1 (February 2016): 74–89.

28. Nayak, Chetan S., and Arayamparambil C. Anilkumar. "EEG Normal Waveforms." In *StatPearls [Internet].* Treasure Island, FL: StatPearls Publishing, 2022.

29. Gardner, Gerald, and Aidan A. Kelly. *The Gardnerian Book of Shadows: The Central Sacred Text of Wicca.* n.p., 2019.

30. Lady Sable Aradia. *The Witch's Eight Paths of Power: A Complete Course in Magick and Witchcraft.* San Francisco: Weiser Books, 2014.

31. Kelden. *The Crooked Path: An Introduction to Traditional Witchcraft.* Woodbury, MN: Llewellyn, 2020.

32. Hunter, Devin. *The Witch's Book of Spirits.* Woodbury, MN: Llewellyn, 2017.

33. Murphy-Hiscock, Arin. *The House Witch: Your Complete Guide to Creating a Magical Space with Rituals and Spells for Hearth and Home.* Avon, MA: Adams Media, 2018.

34. Kelly, Aidan. "About Naming Ostara, Litha, and Mabon." Patheos, May 2, 2017. https://www.patheos.com/blogs/aidankelly/2017/05/naming-ostara-litha-mabon/.

35. Green, Marian. *The Elements of Natural Magic.* Dorset, England: Element Books, 1997.

36. Gottesdiener, Sarah Faith. *The Moon Book: Lunar Magic to Change Your Life.* New York: St. Martin's Essentials, 2020.

37. Kynes, Sandra. *Sea Magic: Connecting with the Ocean's Energy.* Woodbury, MN: Llewellyn, 2008.

38. Xie, Y., Q. Tang, G. Chen, M. Xie, S. Yu, J. Zhao, and L. Chen, "New Insights into the Circadian Rhythm and Its Related Diseases." *Frontiers in Physiology* 10 (June 2019).

39. Serin, Yeliz, and Nilüfer Acar Tek. "Effect of Circadian Rhythm on Metabolic Processes and the Regulation of Energy Balance." *Annals of Nutrition and Metabolism* 74, no. 4 (June 2019): 322–30.

40. Helfrich-Förster, C., S. Monecke, I. Spiousas, T. Hovestadt, O. Mitesser, and T. A. Wehr. "Women Temporarily Synchronize Their Menstrual Cycles with the Luminance and Gravimetric Cycles of the Moon." *Science Advances* 7, no. 5 (January 2021): 113–31.

41. Wachter, Aidan. *Six Ways: Approaches & Entries for Practical Magic.* n.p.: Red Temple Press, 2018.

42. Zakroff, Laura Tempest. *Weave the Liminal: Living Modern Traditional Witchcraft.* Woodbury, MN: Llewellyn, 2019.

43. Cunningham, Scott. *Earth, Air, Fire & Water: More Techniques of Natural Magic.* Woodbury, MN: Llewellyn, 1991.

44. Cunningham, Scott. *Earth Power: Techniques of Natural Magic.* Woodbury, MN: Llewellyn, 1983.

45. Penczak, Christopher. *The Outer Temple of Witchcraft: Circles, Spells and Rituals.* Woodbury, MN: Llewellyn, 2013.

46. Chamberlain, Lisa. *Wicca Elemental Magic: A Guide to the Elements, Witchcraft, and Magic Spells.* n.p.: Chamberlain Publications, 2014.

47. Araujo, Bernardo B. A., Luiz Gustavo R. Oliveira-Santos, Matheus S. Lima-Ribeiro, José Alexandre F. Diniz-Filho, and Fernando A. S. Fernandez. "Bigger Kill Than Chill: The Uneven Roles of Humans and Climate on Late Quaternary Megafaunal Extinctions." *Quaternary International* 413 (February 2017): 216–22.

48. Surovell, Todd A., Spencer R. Pelton, Richard Anderson-Sprecher, and Adam D. Myers. "Test of Martin's Overkill Hypothesis Using Radiocarbon Dates on Extinct Megafauna." *Proceedings of the National Academy of Sciences* 113 (2016): 889–891.

49. Sandom, Christopher, Søren Faurby, Brody Sandel, and Jens-Christian Svenning. "Global Late Quaternary Megafauna Extinctions Linked to Humans, Not Climate Change." *Proceedings of the Royal Society B: Biological Sciences* 113, no. 4 (January 2016): 886–91.

50. Wroe, Stephen, Judith Field, Richard Fullagar, and Lars S. Jermin. "Megafaunal Extinction in the Late Quaternary and the Global Overkill Hypothesis." *Alcheringa* 28 (2004): 291–331.

51. Djoghlaf, Ahmed. "U.N. Convention on Biological Diversity." Message from Mr. Ahmed Djoghlaf, Executive Secretary, on the occasion of the International Day for Boiological Diversity. Quebec, 2007.

52. Bailey, Michael D. *Historical Dictionary of Witchcraft.* Oxford: The Scarecrow Press, Inc., 2003.

53. Boracchia, Marina. "What We Lost at the Stake: Witch Hunts and the Production of Femininities' Subjectivity and Sexuality." *El lugar sin límites* 1, no. 2 (October 2019): 7–19.

54. Mortali, Micah. *Rewilding: Meditations, Practices, and Skills for Awakening in Nature.* Boulder, CO: Sounds True, 2019.

55. Lecouteux, Claude. *Demons and Spirits of the Land: Ancestral Lore and Practices.* Rochester, VT: Inner Traditions, 2015.

56. Horne, Roger J. *Folk Witchcraft: A Guide to Lore, Land & the Familiar Spirit for the Solitary Practitioner.* n.p.: Moon over the Mountain Press, 2021.

57. Illes, Judika. *Encyclopedia of Spirits: The Ultimate Guide to the Magic of Fairies, Genies, Demons, Ghosts, Gods & Goddesses.* New York: HarperOne, 2009.

58. Grimassi, Raven. *Communing with the Ancestors: Your Spirit Guides, Bloodline Allies, and the Cycle of Reincarnation.* Newburyport, MA: Weiser Books, 2016.

59. Vaudoise, Mallorie. *Honoring Your Ancestors: A Guide to Ancestral Veneration.* Woodbury, MN: Llewellyn, 2019.

60. Dionne, Danielle. *Magickal Mediumship: Partnering with the Ancestors for Healing and Spiritual Development.* Woodbury, MN: Llewellyn, 2020.

61. Delaforge, Gaetan. "The Templar Tradition: Yesterday and Today." *Gnosis Magazine* 6, 1987.

62. Faerywolf, Storm. *Forbidden Mysteries of Faery Witchcraft.* Woodbury, MN: Llewellyn, 2018.

63. Pradas, Lidia. *The Complete Grimoire: Magickal Practices and Spells for Awakening Your Inner Witch.* Beverly, MA: Fair Winds Press, 2020.

64. Mankey, Jason, and Laura Tempest Zakroff. *The Witch's Altar: The Craft, Lore & Magick of Sacred Space.* Woodbury, MN: Llewellyn, 2018.

65. Serith, Ceisiwr. *The Big Book of Pagan Prayer and Ritual.* Newburyport, MA: Weiser Books, 2020.

66. Vernant, Jean-Pierre. "Hestia–Hermes: The Religious Expression of Space and Movement among the Greeks." *Social Science Information* 8, no. 4 (August 1969): 131–68.

67. Ward, Terence P., ed. *First and Last: A Devotional for Hestia.* n.p.: Bibliotheca Alexandrina, 2017.

68. Kiernan, Anjou. *The Book of Altars and Sacred Spaces: How to Create Magical Spaces in Your Home for Ritual and Intention.* Beverly, MA: Fair Winds Press, 2020.

69. Grimassi, Raven. *Encyclopedia of Wicca & Witchcraft.* St. Paul, MN: Llewellyn, 2000.

70. Penczak, Christopher. *The Witch's Heart: The Magick of Perfect Love & Perfect Trust.* Woodbury, MN: Llewellyn, 2011.

71. Henshilwood, Christopher. "The Origins of Symbolism, Spirituality, and Shamans: Exploring Middle Stone Age Material Culture in South Africa." In Becoming Human: Innovation in Prehistoric Material and Spiritual Culture, edited by Colin Renfrew and Iain Morley, 29–49. Cambridge: Cambridge University Press, 2009. 29–49.

72. Zakroff, Laura Tempest. *Sigil Witchery: A Witch's Guide to Crafting Magick Symbols.* Woodbury, MN: Llewellyn, 2018.

73. Hunter, Devin. *The Witch's Book of Mysteries.* Woodbury, MN: Llewellyn, 2019.

74. Penczak, Christopher. *Instant Magick: Ancient Wisdom, Modern Spellcraft.* Woodbury, MN: Llewellyn, 2005.

75. Murphy-Hiscock, Arin. *The Green Witch: Your Complete Guide to the Natural Magic of Herbs, Flowers, Essential Oils, and More.* Avon, MA: Adams Media, 2017.

76. Maddox, Kelly-Ann. *Rebel Witch: Carve the Craft that's Yours Alone.* London: Watkins, 2021.

Acknowledgments

I would have thought that the fear of facing a blank page would have faded by my third book, but it hasn't. The possibilities of what to write are infinite, which can be scary.

I want to acknowledge everybody that helped me overcome that feeling: my always supportive family, my encouraging publishing and editing team, the witchcraft authors that came before me, the wonderful Wiccan Tips community, and, of course, you, the reader. Thank you.

Finally, I have to mention the person in charge of the other half of my books, Nata Vedana, the illustrator. Without her art, my books would be incomplete.

About the Author

Lidia Pradas is the Wiccan witch behind the Instagram sensation Wiccan Tips and the author of *The Complete Grimoire*. She was born in Spain and comes from a family of witches who taught her Celtic pagan traditions. Lidia writes and teaches about witchcraft and paganism, and she is dedicated to helping beginner witches find their own Wiccan path.

About the Illustrator

Nata Vedana is a self-taught artist and illustrator with an authentic style who finds her inspiration in the dark aesthetics, gothic subculture, and modern witchcraft practices. She spent her childhood in a picturesque little town at the seaside that was full of legends and myths.

From a young age, she got carried away by the scary tales of the Grimm brothers and by the stories of Edgar Allan Poe, H. P. Lovecraft, and Anne Rice. All this has influenced her art.

Today, Nata is a practicing witch and pagan, and she is the designer and mastermind of Pandora Witch Shop, an online store popular with witches all over the globe that specializes in creating original witchcraft tools and attributes.

Nata works with different media like watercolor, acrylic and oil painting, ink, and digital art. Her main purpose in life is constant development, bringing to life her original ideas and creating something excitingly new.

Today she lives in Kyiv, Ukraine, along with her special ones and her beloved black cat.

INDEX